—African-American Biographies—

DUKE ELLINGTON

Giant of Jazz

Series Consultant:
Dr. Russell L. Adams, Chairman
Department of Afro-American Studies, Howard University

Wendie C. Old

Enslow Publishers, Inc.

40 Industrial Road	PO Box 38
Box 398	Aldershot
Berkeley Heights, NJ 07922	Hants GU12 6BP
USA	UK

http://www.enslow.com

For Mercer Ellington, 1919-1996

Library of Congress Cataloging-in-Publication Data

Old, Wendie C.
    Duke Ellington, giant of jazz / Wendie C. Old.
       p. cm. — (African-American biographies)
    Includes bibliographical references (p.) and index.
    Summary: Examines the life and career of the talented jazz composer,
bandleader, and pianist, from his childhood in Washington, D.C., through his
battle against racism, to his influence on the world of jazz.
    ISBN 0-89490-691-7
    1. Ellington, Duke, 1899-1974—Juvenile literature. 2. Jazz musicians—
United States—Biography—Juvenile literature. 3. Afro-American musicians—
Biography—Juvenile literature.
    [1. Ellington, Duke, 1899-1974. 2. Musicians. 3. Composers.
4. Afro-Americans— Biography.] I. Title. II. Series.
ML3930.E44043   1996
781.65'092—dc20   96-3279
                                                   CIP
                                           AC MN

Printed in the United States of America

10 9 8 7 6 5 4 3

Illustration Credits:
Duke Ellington Collection, National Museum of American History,
Smithsonian Institution, pp. 17, 20, 42, 67, 70, 88, 90, 95, 97, 106, 111,
115; photograph by Wendie C. Old, pp. 29, 31, 40, 109, 113; Ruth
Ellington Boatwright Collection, National Museum of American History,
Smithsonian Institution, pp. 33, 53, 64, 72, 99, 102.

Cover Illustration:
Duke Ellington Collection, National Museum of American History,
Smithsonian Institution

CONTENTS

1

BORN AGAIN

In the early 1950s, the music world whispered, "Duke Ellington? His band was the greatest—*once upon a time*. [He just] hasn't got it anymore."[1] Ellington and his band members either had to defeat that rumor or fade away.

They hoped to regain national recognition by accepting an invitation to perform at a brand new event in summer concerts—the outdoor musical festival.

The summer band concert in the city park had been a staple of American life since the turn of the century. But there had been no place celebrating the only true American music, jazz, until 1954 when the first Newport American Jazz Festival was held in Newport, Rhode Island.

The idea was developed by George Wein, the owner of a small Boston jazz club. He convinced millionaire Louis Lorillard to help him promote the jazz festival in Freebody Park near the huge summer homes owned by the extremely rich of Boston and New York.

They invited the top jazz performers in the nation, from southern jazz bands who called themselves Dixielanders to small modern jazz quartets. The excitement of listening to all these artists in one place drew enthusiastic fans from all walks of life. If Ellington and his orchestra could sparkle in this setting, no one could accuse them of being has-beens again.

Ellington was more than just a bandleader and the conductor of fifteen talented musicians. He was the composer and arranger of the jazz music his orchestra performed. In addition, he played a little piano (as he modestly referred to his own contribution in the group), often leading the group from his piano stool.

Leading a big band is a business. Ellington sometimes also acted as manager for the group, finding jobs or gigs where they could perform. However, during the early 1950s, most of the big bands were breaking up because of the lack of gigs. People were not going to dances, filling movie houses, attending concerts, or going to vaudeville shows—the venues that used to hire the big bands. People were staying home watching a new invention called television. Advertising dollars that had supported band and orchestra concerts on radio now fed television shows. Radio stations found they could save money playing prerecorded music. Television was not interested in jazz performers. Television had decided that other types of music from classical to rock and roll had more public appeal.

Ellington's orchestra found themselves bouncing from one one-night stand to another. Here a concert, there a dance, but no long-term gig paying enough to support fifteen musicians. Ellington often had to pay their salaries out of his own income from the sale of records.

Even though jazz was finally being taken seriously in colleges—studied and analyzed by music students—when colleges looked for performers to entertain their students, they invited smaller groups like those of Miles Davis and Dave Brubeck, not large bands like Duke Ellington's.

Ellington refused to lay off musicians during the times he could not find work for them. "The only reason we're still in it [the music business] is mainly artistic interest," Ellington said. "We're not one of those people who stay in the business only so long as business is good. We stay in it 52 weeks a year."[2]

Besides, he needed the group. He needed to have them around in order to hear how his latest compositions sounded. He did not just write music. He wrote music for the particular instrumentalists in his orchestra. For example, if Cat Anderson could hit particularly high notes on his trumpet, Ellington wrote a section for him to shine.

He also loved the performing aspect of his music. He needed the challenge of winning the next audience. He loved being theatrical and putting on a show.[3]

By 1955, Ellington grabbed any musical gig he could find. The lowest point came when the group played mood music for several weeks for the Aquacades, a water show in Queens, New York. Ellington was not even hired as the conductor. The show hired his orchestra. Ellington played a medley of his hits on the piano, then left.

Despite this low period, Ellington could not stop composing. He used the free time to write a musical play, *The Man with Four Sides*. However, it was never performed during his lifetime.

The critics panned the show at the Aquacades, declaring that Ellington had descended to merely being "a footnote to the history of jazz."[4]

His son, Mercer, said:

> . . . it looked like there might not be another way to come back. It looked like he might not be able to

continue to help other people, relatives and friends, as he had throughout his life. . . . He was in management difficulties, public recognition seemed to be diminishing, and he was worried.[5]

In April of 1956, *Time* magazine interviewed him for a cover story to be published later in the summer celebrating his twenty-five years as a nationally known musician. This would make him the sixteenth African American to be on the cover of *Time* magazine. Ellington hoped the magazine would emphasize that he was still active as a musician/composer, not simply feature his historical fame. "No matter how bad things got, [Ellington] never dwelt on them, but continued to look at what he was about to do."[6]

That year he planned to rise from the ashes at the Newport Jazz Festival of 1956. He and his orchestra had not been invited as the headliner of the show. Instead, they were invited to represent the older type of big jazz band.

In addition to the current star jazz performers, all the important people of the jazz world would be in the audience: record company executives, promoters, music publishers, magazine reviewers, and newspaper columnists and photographers, along with dedicated jazz fans.

Ellington's record company, Columbia Records, had agreed to record his performance live at Newport. Failure or success, this attempt would be etched on vinyl for posterity. He was still backstage negotiating the fine points of the record deal at 8:30 P.M. when his band began their first set of the evening. The orchestra normally began playing "Take the 'A' Train" (Ellington's theme song) without him. Ellington would bound onto the stage, conduct the last few bars of the tune, then introduce the bandmembers and continue the concert. This evening, when he went on stage, he discovered the group was missing four players—not a good start for a comeback.

After a few melodic pieces, the orchestra made way for other jazz bands. The modern jazz groups that followed entertained with a cool, intellectual style. The audience clapped politely but with little enthusiasm. Ellington and his bandmembers settled down backstage for a three-hour wait until their next set. However, each succeeding jazz group took more time than they were allotted.

It was a cold, moonless evening. The festival was scheduled to end at midnight. The last group did not take the stage until 11:15 P.M., which pushed Ellington's entrance back to 11:45 P.M. As his orchestra began to set up their layout, the audience of ten thousand prepared to head for their cars. Ellington, seeing them go, grew testy. "What are we—the animal act, the acrobats?"[7] he grumbled to Wein. As an old veteran of vaudeville, he was acquainted with the policy of putting a lesser act of animals or tumblers to close the show while the audience left the theater. It was known as an exit act.

He had no intention of being an exit act. He had carefully planned this comeback, composing a special piece just for tonight and ending with a piece that sparkled. The orchestra was raring to go. Paul Gonsalves remembers how the bandmembers were feeling about this gig. "There was a real competitive feeling in the band that night, and we went out there to play the very best we could. After all the little groups, the impact of a big band is what you want for a festival's [grand] finale."[8]

The audience sat respectfully during Ellington's brand new "Newport Jazz Festival Suite," but more left during the breaks between the next few pieces of music. Only seven thousand remained when Ellington called for his last scheduled piece, "Diminuendo and Crescendo in Blue." It consisted of two sections performed by the full orchestra held together by a brief tenor saxophone solo. It had been composed in 1937. The current band members had only played it once before. In fact, the soloist, Paul Gonsalves, claims he had not known it was going to be included at Newport until right before he went on stage.

Ellington took him aside and told him, "When we get through the first part, you go out there and play as long as you like."[9]

Gonsalves knew how to play just the right amount

of time to build up crowd excitement. This usually meant about six or seven choruses.

The audience sat up and took notice at the opening section of "Diminuendo and Crescendo in Blue." Ellington grabbed the theme from the band and pounded the piano keys while Gonsalves made his way down front. Driven by the steady, rocking beat of drummer San Woodyard and bassist Jimmy Woode, Gonsalves produced a sound so exotic people stopped in the very act of passing through the exits. People moving up the aisles turned back.

Gonsalves stayed on top of the beat, varying his technique with every chorus. The drummer and bassist drove the beat even stronger. The whole band seemed to pulse with the feeling. They were swinging. With each chorus, Gonsalves built up the excitement, the urgency in his playing.[10]

The audience snapped their fingers, then clapped their hands with the beat. Many began to shout for more. Something unexpected was happening on stage, and the whole audience was pulsing with it. By the seventh chorus, a blond girl in a black dress danced over in one of the expensive box seats. Others began to dance by their seats or in the aisles. By the tenth chorus, the crowd was roaring. Most were standing, egging the band on.

On stage, Ellington pushed the band to higher and higher crescendos. One bandmember recalled,

"Duke was really out there doin' it. 'Ah-HAH! Come on! *Yeah!* . . .' He was almost dancing . . . hand-clapping and hollerin' 'Ah-HAH!'"[11] The recording of that performance captures most of this.

Some of the drummers of the other jazz bands stood by the side, pounding the beat on the elevated stage with their hands or rolled up newspapers, cheering them on.

George Wein, standing in the wings, yelled to Ellington, trying to get him to stop for fear of causing a riot. Ellington shook his finger at Wein and yelled back, "Don't be rude to the artists!"[12] He was in full control of the excitement. Stopping was more likely to cause a riot than continuing on.

Gonsalves continued. For twenty-seven choruses, he blew on his horn, eyes shut, concentrating on living the music. Then as the crowd worked to a climax, he threw the theme back to the band. Ellington picked it up with a brief, swinging piano solo. Then the whole orchestra took over for a rocking conclusion with Cat Anderson's high-pitched trumpeting sounding over all.

The crowd would not let them go. They cheered, stomped their feet, and yelled for more, enthusiastically demanding encores. Ellington called for two quieter tunes, "I Got It Bad" and "Jeep's Blues." The audience still would not let them go. Ellington's orchestra played two more. About 1:30 A.M., he finally got the crowd settled down enough to let him off the stage, throwing kisses to the audience and shouting his traditional closing line, "We love you madly."

Don George, Ellington's friend, remembers, "Everybody was very excited . . . kissing everybody else . . . throwing our arms around each other. Duke looked drained but happy. Everyone was smiling, smiling, smiling."[13]

Word spread throughout the music world. The nearly fifty-eight-year-old Ellington was back on top of the world of jazz. The recording made that night became Ellington's biggest selling record. Other people his age were looking forward to retirement, but not Ellington. If asked, he would reply, "Retire to what?"[14] His later years were the most productive of all.

He insisted, "I was born in 1956 at the Newport festival."[15]

2

FAMILY

 dward Kennedy (Duke) Ellington confessed in his autobiography, *Music Is My Mistress*, ". . . I was pampered and pampered, and spoiled rotten by all the women in the family."[1] Since both his mother and father came from large families, there were many aunts and female cousins to help his mother do this pampering.

His father, James Edward Ellington (otherwise known as J.E.), and his mother, Daisy Kennedy, were both born in the same year—1879—but not in the same state. J.E. was born on April 15 in Lincolntown,

🔲🔲🔲🔲🔲🔲🔲🔲🔲🔲🔲🔲🔲🔲🔲🔲🔲🔲🔲🔲🔲🔲🔲🔲🔲🔲🔲🔲🔲🔲🔲🔲🔲🔲

North Carolina, and Daisy was born on January 4 in
Washington, D.C. J.E. was the second youngest of a
family of fourteen. Daisy had nine brothers and sisters
in her family.

These aunts and uncles also had large families.
Thus many cousins ran in and out of J.E. and Daisy's
house. Ellington describes these cousins as being ". . . a
strong racial mixture, black and white and bronze and
sepia, brown, yellow and all the other magnificent
shades and tints of human pigmentation."[2]

Daisy's first child died soon after it was born. During Daisy's second pregnancy, the twenty-year-old
Ellingtons stayed at Daisy's father's house on 20th
Street, a middle-class African-American section in
Washington, D.C. The Great Blizzard of 1899 blew
drifting snow, piling it up to their second story window.

Like many children at the turn of the century, Edward was not born at a hospital. He was born on April
29, 1899, in his grandfather's house.

Daisy and her four sisters hovered over young
Edward to make sure he would survive and grow.
Since Edward's sister, Ruth, was not born until he was
sixteen years old, he enjoyed all the rights and
privileges of an only child throughout most of his
youth. Along with these privileges came the handicap
of a hovering, overprotective, loving mother.

If he were to get sick, the doctor was called

Edward Ellington, the young Duke, was already regal at age four.

immediately. At age four, he caught pneumonia. Daisy called two doctors. She stayed by his bedside until he recovered. She was not going to lose this child. During Edward's first years of school, his mother followed him there and was waiting at the school door to walk him home. Ellington remembers, "She didn't think I saw her, but I did."[3]

Daisy taught him that nothing was beyond his reach. She taught him that he was special.

J.E.'s family had moved from North Carolina (a segregated state) to Washington, D.C., when he was young. When they arrived, they discovered the color line in Washington, D.C., home of one of the largest African-American communities in the United States, was just as unbreakable as the one in their home state. Certain jobs were not open to African Americans at the turn of the century.

On the African-American side of the color line, social status was determined by the jobs you held. Intelligence was respected. Those who had succeeded in becoming doctors, lawyers, teachers, and ministers were on a higher social level than servants and street cleaners. Those people who worked for doctors were socially higher than others of the African-American community who held more menial jobs.

J.E. and his closest brother, George, trained to be butlers. George entered the catering business, but J.E. worked for Dr. M. F. Cuthbert, a white doctor who lived on the fashionable part of Rhode Island Avenue. He became Dr. Cuthbert's confidant and close friend.

Dr. Cuthbert was the physician for important families in the nation's capitol, including several presidents. He gave the Ellington family the same kind of medical care as he did the president of the United States. In addition, whenever the White House needed a temporary butler, he recommended J.E. for the job. Even after J.E. changed jobs and worked in the Navy's blueprinting office, he would moonlight as a butler, helping with the family catering business that George had started with another brother.

J.E. was an even-tempered " . . . happy man who enjoyed all the pleasures life provided him, who relaxed easily and didn't let anything worry him very much."[4] He had a " . . . courtly manner, teasing wit and fondness for fine things and elegant clothes."[5]

Edward's mother, Daisy Kennedy Ellington, a lovely, soft-spoken African-American woman, did most of the worrying for the family. She was the daughter of a Washington, D.C., police officer and grew up into " . . . a woman of rigorous moral principle. . . ."[6] She had a prim manner and frowned upon cosmetics— even lipstick. She, unlike her husband, graduated from high school.

All of the extended family helped with George's catering business. Because of the family's connection to Dr. Cuthbert and their experience with Uncle

Edward's beautiful mother, Daisy Ellington, did most of the worrying for the family.

George's catering business, the Ellingtons lived better than most of the African Americans in the city and a good many of the middle-class white people.

For example, whenever the rich, white families' sets of good dishes were reduced from twelve place settings to ten or less because of missing or broken dishes, they would purchase fresh new sets and offer the short sets to the people who worked for them as servants, such as the caterers. The same thing happened with shorts sets of crystal, damaged silverware, and other damaged items such as figurines.

The Ellingtons dined off good china and silver. They enjoyed the good food left over from the parties the wonderful cooks of the family helped cater. Naturally, by the time Edward was in his teens, he knew all the names of quality china, crystal glasses, and silver. He had observed how to live well. Duke Ellington's son, Mercer, said, "This, you might say, is where the dukedom began—his experience of being around at a time when his father was working for very splendid people."[7]

Because of his training as a butler, J.E. had gracious manners, and he taught them to his son. He dressed well and made sure his son wore good quality clothing. As he matured, Edward also copied his father's impeccable English and his gracious manner toward women.

However, to young Ellington, baseball rated higher

than girls. "After all, baseball, football, track, and athletics were what the real he-men were identified with," Ellington explained, "and so they were naturally the most important to me."[8] He and his friends played ball in a park on Sixteenth Street not far from the White House—close enough that when President Theodore Roosevelt exercised his horse, he would pass their baseball game. Sometimes he would pause to watch them play, then wave as he trotted away.

The long walks Edward took with his cousins all over the city to visit various relatives kept him in shape for his athletics. The food they offered him was enough to satisfy even a growing boy. Ellington remembers that all of his aunts were wonderful cooks, famous for their cakes and freezers of ice cream.

Daisy raised Edward with love, praise, and encouragement. She insisted that nothing was beyond his reach. This did wonders for his sense of self. He kept that feeling of being a favored person for the rest of his life.[9]

He read books, especially pulp westerns, detective stories, and all the Sherlock Holmes tales he could find.

During a baseball game one day, Edward was talking on the sidelines when another boy went up to bat. His friend hit a long drive and let his bat fly as he ran for first base. Instead of falling to the ground, the bat flew into his waiting teammates, bonking the back of Edward's head.

Unfortunately, Edward's mother saw it happen. She scooped him up and swept him to the doctor. In order to get him off the street and back inside where it was safe, Daisy decided Edward should take piano lessons.

Before the invention of radio and television, people entertained each other in the evenings and guests on Sunday. Middle-class families kept a piano in the house for this purpose. Edward's mother often played the piano for her own enjoyment as well as that of the family and guests. His father picked out operatic music on the piano by ear and sang barbershop quartets with friends. As a result, Edward grew up with music constantly around him.

They hired a piano teacher for him.

Ellington remembered:

> My piano teacher, Mrs. [Marietta] Clinkscales (that was really her name), got paid several times a week . . . for these lessons, but I missed more than I took, because of my enthusiasm for playing ball, and running and racing through the street.[10]

When Edward disappeared, a good part of his extended family was enlisted to find the runaway piano student. The Northwest streets of the middle class African-American neighborhood would ring with the calls, "Edward, Edward, where are you?"[11]

Edward never did learn the piece he was required to play at the end of the year recital. Mrs. Clinkscales had to sit with him and play the high notes while Edward played the rhythm notes at the bottom end of the piano. Some years later, when Edward was a teenager, it was these rhythmic lower notes that attracted him to popular music.

3

ART OR MUSIC?
MUSIC OR ART?

---

ecause of Edward Ellington's involvement in sports and lack of interest in academic subjects at Garrison Junior High, he collected average to poor grades. They were not good enough to allow him to attend the more prestigious African-American high school, Dunbar High, in 1914.

As a young African-American man in a world with few jobs open to African Americans, he knew it was important for him to find a way to make a living.[1] He entered Armstrong Technical High School, a vocational high school. In this school he could take freehand and mechanical drawing courses to prepare himself for a career in commercial art.

His friends all had nicknames for each other. Through the years, he earned quite a few, including Cutey, Stinkpot, the Phony Duke, and finally just plain Duke.

He deliberately lived up to that nickname. He enjoyed dressing well but was not flashy. He dressed to look smart and attractive. He was a sheik, a term that became popular after a movie star played the part of a desert sheik who was irresistible to women. Daisy encouraged his tendency to be extremely neat, sending him off to school with firm creases in his trousers (even if those trousers had been mended with patches), with a perfectly knotted tie, and with his shoes always shined.

He presented himself with style. He grew tall and self-confident, striding forward with a regal gait that he perfected in high school and kept lifelong. His strong voice commanded attention.[2] He looked like an aristocrat. He looked and acted like a duke.

His high school chum, Edgar McEntree, (who Ellington remembered in his autobiography as being high society and popular, and who also liked to dress well) made the "Duke" nickname official.

The summer before he entered Armstrong Technical, Duke and his mother spent their annual summer seaside vacation in Asbury Park, New Jersey, on the Atlantic Ocean. He and a group of his friends heard of a dishwasher job available in a nearby hotel. They all raced to apply for it. Duke ran fastest and got the job.

After he was hired, Bowser, the previous year's dishwasher who had been newly promoted to head-waiter, took Duke under his wing. They grew to be friends. They had long talks about life and music as they worked over the hot, soapy tub.

The popular music of the day was ragtime, a fast-paced music that made everyone want to bounce, clap, and dance along. Despite Duke's unsuccessful piano lessons years ago, he became interested in this new music.

Bowser told him, "Man, in Philadelphia they've got a young piano player called Harvey Brooks. He's just about your age. You ought to hear him play. He's terrific."[3]

At the end of the summer, Bowser and the fourteen-year-old Duke stopped off in Philadelphia to hear Brooks. Duke remembered:

> He was swinging and he had a tremendous left hand, and when I got home I had a real yearning to play. I hadn't been able to get off the ground before, but after hearing him I said to myself, "Man, you're just going to *have* to do it!"[4]

The ragtime beat focused strong accents on the usual weak beats in music and vice versa. Instead of the normal ONE/two/THREE/four rhythm, the syncopated beat of ragtime became one/TWO/three/FOUR.

Scott Joplin, known as the "King of Ragtime Composers," wrote the first hit ragtime song, the "Maple Leaf Rag."[5] (Another Joplin song, "The Entertainer," became popular again in the 1970s when it became the theme music for the film *The Sting*.)

The walking bass, which Duke first saw performed with Brooks' tremendous left hand, created an incessant repetition, going up and down the chords in the same pattern, over and over. This pattern of jumping back and forth was called "stride."

Home in Washington, he attempted the stride technique on the piano. He consulted several formal music teachers but found he just could not learn that way. He discovered he picked up more music instruction over at Frank Holiday's pool room on T Street, next to the Howard Theater, just listening to the professional and amateur piano players who gathered there. Some of the pros could read music and some could not—managing to get along playing by ear.

Duke explained, "There were things I wanted to do that were not in books. . . . I was always lucky enough to run into people who had the answer."[6] He said, "I was a great listener!"[7] The musicians at Frank Holiday's pool room demonstrated their techniques and talked him through the lessons. "[This] was the birth of my primitive system of memorizing," Duke said. "[It] is more or less what I still depend upon."[8]

At home, Duke practiced his musical skills, the old

Frank Holiday's pool room, where Duke received his musical education, is still standing, but the building is now abandoned.

scales from his elementary school day lessons, combined with new information as he learned it. One week a cold forced him to stay home from school. He grew bored and played with chords at his piano. Gradually his fiddling around congealed into his first musical composition. He decided to name it for his part-time, after-school job. He worked as a soda jerk at the nearby Poodle Dog Cafe, selling sodas and other soft drinks behind the soda fountain counter. He called his first composition "The Soda Fountain Rag."

One day the pianist at the Poodle Dog Cafe was too drunk to perform. Duke took his place and played his one composition. He played it as ragtime. He played it as a one-step, as a two-step, a waltz, a foxtrot, with slow, middle, and fast tempo. The audience never knew it was the same piece of music.

He spent his high school years studying art in school and piano after school. Too often he whiled the time away in his academic classes drumming on table tops or playing on an imaginary keyboard on his classroom desk.

His physical education teacher, Ed Henderson, would yell, "Boy, . . . you're never going to amount to anything as long as you live."[9] For years, Henderson told this tale to new high school students, admitting that he "really had to eat his words."[10]

Duke just smiled. None of the teacher's dire predictions bothered him. He "always felt he would be a success."[11]

One day his friend Edgar McEntree pulled Duke into a senior class party in the gym, announcing that the Duke was a pianist who would not object if asked to play. The seniors loved "The Soda Fountain Rag" and his second composition, "What You Gonna Do When the Bed Breaks Down?"

The next day, as Duke told the story, three of the "prettiest little girls you ever saw" stood in front of

Duke Ellington grew up in this house, owned by his father, at 1212 T Street in Washington, D.C.

his house. One of them yelled up, "Mrs. Ellington. Is Edward ready?"

"Yes, honey," his mother answered, "he'll be right down."[12]

When Duke met them downstairs, they slipped their arms in his and dragged him to a Hop (dance) at Ina Fowlers' house. It was his first experience at skipping school to enjoy a musical party, but not his last.

He quickly learned that sitting down at the piano was a good way to get people, especially girls, to pay attention to him.[13] Suddenly sports were no longer his main interest, because " . . . when you were playing piano, there was always a pretty girl standing at the bass clef end of the piano. I ain't been no athlete since."[14]

Like many teenage boys, Duke thought that having a good time was more important than anything else.[15] For Duke, music was simply part of having a good time. He did just enough homework to get by.

He remained close to his mother but did not tell her everything he did—from his visits to the burlesque shows to his musical education in the local pool room. He certainly did not share his sudden interest in girls and music with her. His grades slipped, but he learned many show business techniques at the theater that he used later in life.

He looked around for mentors to help him learn how to compose. His best mentor was his high school music teacher, Henry Grant, an important figure in

Duke Ellington's little sister, Ruth, was born when he was sixteen years old.

the African-American music circles of Washington, D.C. Grant invited Duke into his home for private lessons in music theory, harmony, and composition. He "remembers Duke as a very good student, who grasped . . . melody and harmony—very easily. . . . Harmonizing a simple melody was always an experiment in color with Duke; it was always important . . . to create a sound that 'rang'. . . ."[16] Already Duke was mixing his love of art with his love of music.

Duke was beginning to absorb the African-American culture around him and incorporate it into his compositions. "I could . . . hear people whistling, and I got all the Negro music that way. You can't learn that in any school."[17]

The musicians from Frank Holiday's pool room never asked for payment. Oliver "Doc" Perry told Duke about a quick method of determining which chords the left hand should use while his right hand was tickling the keys with the melody and how to find that melody on sheet music. Although it was not exactly reading music, it did enable Duke to quickly pick up the styles of any band to which he was assigned, insuring that his piano blended right in. Duke called Doc "my piano parent."[18]

His first professional engagement was for a private party in a room at the True Reformer's Hall. He played four hours without a break. His pay was seventy-five cents. Duke remembered, "I rushed all the way home to my mother with it. But I could not touch a piano key for weeks after—not till my raw fingers had healed again."[19]

Another gig found him playing for a magician/fortune teller. Duke discovered he could ad-lib musical phrases to match the various serious and mystic moods of the performance.

In his senior year, he had advanced enough musically to make good money as a relief player. He had a definite flair for showmanship. He copied the styles of different piano players, making them uniquely his own. His energetically striding left hand flew up and down the bass keys. During solo runs, he threw his hands up in the air off the keyboard as he bounced along the keys, copying the playing style of the Howard Theater's pianist, Lucky Roberts, showing off the polyrhythms of ragtime piano, popular from 1914 to 1916.

In 1917, before he was scheduled to graduate from high school, Duke entered an NAACP (National Association for the Advancement of Colored People) poster competition. He won a scholarship to one of the country's best art schools, the Pratt Institute of Applied Art in Brooklyn, New York. However, when it looked as if Duke would be shy one credit in French, preventing him from graduating with his class, he dropped out of school. He entered the working world without a high school diploma despite his mother's disapproval and despair.[20]

He never used that art scholarship, but he did continue music studies—observing and learning from as many musicians as possible. Duke had made his decision. In the contest between art and music, art never had a chance. It was to be music, music, music the rest of his life.

4

From Washington to New York City

or a while, Ellington freelanced at night as a piano player. However, he could not support himself that way. He needed a day job. He first worked at the Navy Department as a messenger. Then he transferred to the Navy transportation division. His job was to make all the train reservations for the Navy officers passing through the area. Ellington's knowledge of the schedules of every big train in the country came in handy later when he was crisscrossing the country with his own band.

One evening in 1918, Louis Thomas, who found

gigs for a good many musicians in the Washington, D.C., area, sent Ellington on a job he would never forget. He was to create quiet atmospheric music just under the level of conversation at the exclusive Ashland (Virginia) Country Club, a country club for millionaires. Thomas instructed him to "Collect a hundred dollars and bring me ninety."[1] During the performance, Ellington thought about this. Why should he work four hours for $100 and only take home $10? Ellington gave Thompson his cut of $90 but vowed to serve as his own booking agent from then on.[2]

Once he was hired for a gig with one of Washington, D.C.'s most successful African-American commercial musical groups—Russell Wooding's enormous band. Ellington was to play one of the band's five pianos. At the first performance, Ellington added his own musical interpretation of the score. Wooding disapproved and fired him.

Ellington then formed his own band in order to play the music *he* wanted to play. He had been friends with Otto "Toby" Hardwick since their baseball days together, even though Toby was five years younger. Toby began playing the double bass but was too small to manage the huge instrument. His father had to carry it. Ellington convinced Hardwick to play the C melody saxophone. Soon Hardwick was an essential part of Ellington's musicians.

Duke Ellington married his high school sweetheart, Edna Thompson, on July 2, 1918. His son Mercer was born in 1919. A second son came soon after but did not survive.

In 1919 Ellington arranged for a large, boxed ad in the telephone book advertising:

JAZZ BAND	COLORED MUSICIANS
The Duke's Serenaders	
E. K. ELLINGTON,	
Pianist	
1955 3rd St. N.W.	PHONE: NORTH 8136[3]

Since his ad was just as large as the ads of the other, more experienced bandleaders, he figured people would think he was as good as the others. He was correct. He soon was making money both as a bandleader and as a manager of other bands.

Although he never used that scholarship to Pratt, he did use his art training. He and his friend and partner, Ewell Conway, started a sign painting shop. The nearby Howard Theater was a steady customer, requesting painted backdrops and scenery for the various shows.

In addition, since Ellington used the sign shop's phone number in his ads for his bands, he sweet-talked the callers into ordering their dance signs from

When Duke Ellington married Edna Thompson, he bought this little house at 2728 Sherman Street in Washington, D.C. It was the first house he ever bought.

his shop as well. He worked as an artist by day and as a band manager and performer at night.

Also in 1919, a flashy drummer and a great teller of tales, Sonny Greer, entered Ellington's life. He came from New Jersey. He had played with white bands until he arrived in Washington, D.C., to join a black band performing at the Howard Theater. Ellington and Hardwick enticed him to join their band, now called the Washingtonians. The three men remained friends the rest of their lives. Greer and Ellington were a deadly duo—either one could outtalk anyone.

Greer often told people he loved Ellington from the start. "There was some sort of magnetism to him. . . . When he walks into a strange room, the whole place lights up."[4]

By this time, Ellington had quit the Navy job. He had discovered he could make more money running bands—his own and others—because of the demand for entertainment in post-war Washington, D.C. Eventually, he was making $150 to $200 a week from five bands.[5] (This is equal to over $625 a week in 1990s dollar value.) By 1920, his band and the others he managed were playing at cabarets, fashion shows, beauty contests, dance halls, open-air dance pavilions, and theaters. Also, his sign-painting business was booming.

He used his income to build a ten-room house for Edna, Mercer, and himself. He also bought cars, including a Cadillac before his twenty-first birthday.

Duke Ellington (center) and his band performed at Louis Thomas's cabaret in Washington, D.C., about 1920. With Ellington are (from left to right): Sonny Greer, Bertha Ricks, Mrs. Conaway, and Sterling Conaway.

The whole group was crazy about automobiles. After their evening gigs, they would race their cars through the hot streets of the summers of 1919 through 1922, stopping at clubs to have fun until the wee hours of the morning with the other musicians there.

Toward the end of the year 1922, bandleader Wilbur Sweatman sent a message that he needed Sonny Greer for a gig at a vaudeville house in New York City. Vaudeville was all the rage on stages throughout the United States, and many famous vaudeville houses were located in New York City. (Vaudeville means a live variety show that included singers, dancers, comedy acts, animal trick acts, jugglers, and often acrobats, each act following one another on stage.) Sweatman was famous for playing three clarinets at one time. He wanted Greer to be his drummer, but Greer would not come without Ellington and Hardwick.

In February of 1923, all five of the members of the Washingtonian band came along, leaving their wives and children at home.

The band's job was to warm up the crowd before the vaudeville show and to play background music for the various acts. Ellington found it a bit dull. He admitted, however, that he picked up a lot about the inner workings of show business during this time. Unfortunately, this job only lasted a few weeks. Eventually, Greer was reduced to playing pool for money to support the group.

They looked around for other music jobs but found very few. The Broadway movie houses that were playing silent films did not want bands providing the musical background for the films. They hired symphony orchestras to perform classical music during the show. The Washingtonians were offered one-and two-day gigs at small clubs and pool halls, but the pay was not enough to support them comfortably. Legend has it that one time they were reduced to buying a hot dog and splitting it five ways. However, Ellington later admitted this tale was ". . . more of a gag than the truth."[6]

One day, Ellington found $15 lying in the street. He treated the group to a meal. Then he surprised them with tickets back to Washington. In New York City, they had been newcomers and nobodies. Back in Washington, D.C., the Washingtonians were as popular and successful as they had been before they tried to break into the Big Apple.

However, the idea of performing in New York City remained their goal. That summer they returned to New York City and never looked back.

5

NEW YORK CITY SUCCESS

ometime in June 1923, Fats Waller, a friend of Sonny Greer, sent a message about a possible job in the Big Apple. Greer had played drums in a trio with Thomas "Fats" Waller before coming to Washington and joining Ellington.

"I'm quitting next week," Waller said. "Why don't you all come up to New York and take the job? I'll tell 'em about you."[1]

Ellington handled the band's finances and made the train reservations. They planned to find places to live, then bring their families. Greer and Hardwick went on ahead. Ellington tidied up loose ends in Washington, then followed.

With a job practically promised to them, Ellington spared no expense. He traveled in a first class railroad car and ate an expensive dinner in the train's dining car. Instead of taking the subway, he hired a cab when he arrived at New York City's Pennsylvania Station to carry him uptown to Harlem. Adding in generous tips, he spent most of the group's money by the time he reached 129th Street.

Ellington was greeted by a pair of starving friends. The promised job had been filled by another band.

Friends in the music business helped them get a job as the house band in a popular Harlem nightclub owned by Barron Wilkins.

Later that year, another pianist, Ada "Bricktop" Smith, urged them to apply at the old Hollywood Club on West 49th Street near Broadway. Although it was a basement club, for some reason it kept catching on fire. The owner of the club, reputed to be a gangster, would come up to them after a show and suggest that it would be a good idea if they all took their instruments home that night because there was going to be an accident. It was renamed the Kentucky Club in 1925 after another accidental fire.

Ellington found other mentors among the New York City pianists. He became friends with Fats Waller, James P. Johnson (who wrote "Carolina Shout," one of the first tunes Ellington had memorized), Ada "Bricktop" Smith, and Willie "the Lion" Smith. The Lion's piano-playing style and personality made a big impression on him.[2] Ellington's own piano style was moving closer to the jazz sound that became his trademark.

His son, Mercer, said Ellington was "well aware of the importance of being labeled first class."[3] He hired people to talk about him, spreading the word that he was a rare artist. Those men would walk around the after-hours spots telling people how important Duke Ellington was and how they would enjoy hearing him perform. This word of mouth sales talk really worked.

For some time, Ellington had been composing music but had depended upon others to write it down. One day he sold a song to Fred Fisher. Fisher told Ellington, "Okay. Give me a lead sheet and I'll sign the contract."[4] This was at 4:30 P.M. His office closed at 5:00 P.M. Ellington sat at a table in a nearby room that contained ten small booths filled with ten pianists all banging away on ten pianos. Despite the noise, he managed to sketch out his first lead sheet on time.

Ellington continued to audition his compositions in music publishers' offices. One night he was asked to write the music for a musical play. At that time, he did not know that most people take several months to write the words and music for a musical. He simply stayed up all night writing away. In the morning, he had four songs for a musical he called *Chocolate Kiddies*. The promoter, Jack Robbins, pawned his wife's engagement ring to come up with Ellington's fee of $500. He then took the show to Germany. It played for two years at the Berlin Wintergarten Theater. The promoter returned a millionaire, but Ellington did not get one penny of the profit.[5]

Ellington's success in New York City proved to be too much of a strain on his marriage. Edna Ellington discovered to her dismay that it was not only making music that Duke loved, it was the life of a musician that attracted him.[6] Ellington was associating with socialites, celebrities, gangsters, movie stars, and show girls. He was living at night, sleeping by day.

In late 1923, Edna left her son, Mercer, in Washington with his grandparents to join her husband and become a showgirl with the band. However, she "had a hard time sharing her man with the public," especially women fans.[7] Duke carried a permanent scar on his face where Edna slashed him with a knife during one of their fights.

A few years later, Mercer came to live with his parents in New York City. It was difficult for him to be awake during the day, tiptoeing around sleeping parents who worked nights.

During the time that Ellington worked at the Kentucky Club, he developed the Ellington sound. Building on the low, sweet society music his group usually played quietly under the conversation of the club attendees, he experimented with a louder, more jazzy sound. He encouraged his brass bandmembers to play around with mutes, creating a growling, animal-like sound.

There are three parts to producing that growling sound. First is the sound of the horn itself. Secondly, the musician adds a guttural gargling in the throat, and thirdly, he hums a note to match the music. The musician's mouth shapes the different vowel sounds at the mouthpiece end of the horn, while his hands manipulate a plunger at the bell end producing a wah-wah effect, which makes the horn seem to talk.

Although mutes are a common sight today, available in any music store, in the 1920s the band members experimented with various kinds. They put bent-up tin cans in the bell of their horn or rubber toilet plungers over it to muffle, warp, and change the sound. This ". . . new, raw jungle music"[8] made people think of voices moaning in an exotic tropical jungle at night. It was intriguing and highly original music. As the use of mutes was perfected, Ellington's band members began to use the straight mute in the horn combined with the wah-wah plunger mute cupping the bell.

The original Washingtonian men—Duke Ellington, Otto Hardwick, Arthur Whetsol, and Sonny Greer— were soon joined by others. These bandmembers were to be the core of the Ellington sound for almost fifty years.

Freddie Guy joined the group in 1923, first on banjo and then on guitar, staying until 1949.

Arthur Whetsol, the Washingtonian's original trumpet player, left to attend college but rejoined the band afterward in 1928.

He was temporarily replaced by James "Bubber" Miley, eventually advertised on the band's posters as ". . . Bub Miley, America's Hottest Trumpet Player."[9] Highly influenced by the New Orleans jazz bands, Miley was a master at fingering his trumpet with one hand and using a plunger mute with the other, covering and uncovering the bell of his trumpet, creating the wah-wah sound like that of a blues singer. He and Ellington collaborated on the composition of some of the band's earliest pieces of music.

Another expert with the mutes who helped create the growling, jungle sound of the band was Joe "Tricky Sam" Nanton, who joined the band in 1926. Although his parents came from the West Indies, he was a native New Yorker. He used both the plunger mute and a tiny, pixie mute in the bell of his horn to create unusual sounds—the wail of a newborn baby, the bloodcurdling scream of an enraged tiger, or the soft, eerie cooing of a mourning dove.

Harry Carney was just nineteen years old when he joined the band in 1926. He originally doubled on clarinet and alto sax but eventually settled on the baritone saxophone as his main instrument. He became the musical anchor for the Ellington group with his rich, sonorous tones. He could hold a single note for three or four minutes. Although most woodwind players stop playing to take a breath, Carney perfected the art of inhaling through his nose while blowing into the horn through his mouth. He remained a member of Ellington's band until Ellington died.

Carney's friend, Johnny "Jeep" Hodges joined the group in 1928. Although he also played the clarinet, he was later acclaimed as one of the jazz giants on the sax—playing both the alto and soprano saxophones. Except for a five-year break in the early 1950s, he remained with Ellington until he died in 1970.

Others doubled on clarinet, but Barney Bigard specialized in it. His woody tones flavored every piece he performed. He was a light-skinned New Orleans creole who could read difficult parts easily and soar above the brass without screeching. Ellington sought him out soon after he arrived in New York City in 1927 and hired him immediately. He remained for fourteen years.

The rhythm bass (Ellington's favorite low-note part) was played by Wellman Braud from New Orleans. He used the slap-bass style of playing—pulling a single string up one beat and slapping it (or several strings) down against the finger board on the next.

These men became the core of Ellington's famous band.

The Washingtonians crammed themselves onto the stage in the corner of the Kentucky Club, which measured only five feet between floor and ceiling. There was no room for a piano. Ellington directed and played the piano from the floor of the club. Because it was a place for dancing as well as listening to music, they called themselves a dance orchestra instead of a band. And from then on the Washingtonians referred to themselves as Duke Ellington and his Orchestra.

In the fall of 1926, Ellington met Irving Mills. He and his brother Jack owned a publishing firm that sought out gifted but unknown composers, mostly Jewish or African American. Mills became Ellington's agent.

Mills took over the management of the band, booking their gigs, doing the publicity, arranging recording sessions, and publishing sheets of Ellington's music. Besides taking his percentage from the recording income, Mills also placed his name beside Ellington's as cowriter of some of the songs on which he helped polish the lyrics.

He fit the stereotype of a fast-talking agent waving his cigar wildly around to punctuate his points. While Ellington was tall and dignified, Mills was short, stocky, and argumentative.

Duke Ellington poses for a publicity shot in the mid-1920s. It was about this time that his band changed its name from the Washingtonians to Duke Ellington and his Orchestra.

Mills decided that they both would make more money if Ellington composed all the music the band recorded. Their first important recording was November 29, 1926. Under the name Duke Ellington and His Kentucky Club Orchestra, they recorded four of his songs, including the popular but moody "East St. Louis Toodle-Oo," which Bubber Miley helped write. Ellington used this piece as his theme song until the 1940s. Critics consider it an early masterpiece.[10]

The early recordings were yelled into a funnel-like device that caused a needle to vibrate on the recording medium. By the time Ellington was recording records, the electronic microphone had been invented. This crude device created a lot of hiss and could not reproduce all musical frequencies.

Ellington played with the limitations, discovering where to place his musicians in the recording studio to create the best sound on the recording. No one else thought to push their bass player to the front of the group so its sound could be heard. He balanced the piano and the drummer within the group. The growl trumpet and trombone sounds and the wah-wah created resonances other groups' recordings just did not have. One time, in Chicago doing a recording for RCA, he kept asking the engineers to move the microphone here and there, trying to get exactly the right resonance. Finally they had it. They recorded that piece of music with the microphone in the men's washroom.

Among his many ground-breaking firsts is his being the first to use an echo chamber in recording. He recorded Johnny Hodges's solo in "Empty Ballroom Blues" in an early type of echo chamber. He was the first to make the huge bass violin the mainstay of all jazz orchestras. He featured bassist Wellman Braud in 1928 in the recording of "Hot and Bothered."

He also began composing his music to last precisely three minutes. This was a comfortable length of time for dancing in the clubs in which he performed and also was the exact amount of time needed to fill up a ten-inch 78 rpm (revolutions per minute) record. Many other bands ended their recordings when the song ended, often leaving large blocks of empty space on their records. Ellington never did. In addition, his technically challenging introductions, interludes, and codas encouraged the listener to play his recordings over and over again.

He soon was recording so often that the record companies insisted he use different names. That way each record label could claim they had the exclusive use of a particular musician's talents. The names included:

Duke Ellington on the Victor label
The Jungle Band on the Brunswick label
The Washingtonians on the Harmony label

The Whoopee Makers on the Perfect label
Sonny Greer and His Memphis Men on the Columbia label
The Harlem Footwarmers on the Okeh label[11]

Irving Mills worked hard for all his clients, cracking race barriers. He managed to get Ellington's recordings listed in several white-only catalogs of music.

Ellington's orchestra had really arrived when Mills sent them to try out for the prestigious Cotton Club, Harlem's most fashionable nightspot.

6

THE COTTON CLUB AND ALL THAT JAZZ

arlem was *the* place to be in the 1920s. It was home to the majority of African Americans on the island of Manhattan. It also was the cultural hot spot of the city. Musicians, composers, artists, actors, dancers, and writers created what was to become known as the Harlem Renaissance.

Years later the African-American poet Langston Hughes described what he would have done had he been a rich man during the 1920s. "I would have bought a house in Harlem and built musical steps up to the front door and installed chimes that at the press of a button played Ellington tunes."[1]

This was the era known as the Roaring Twenties. The economy was booming. Girls cut their hair short and adopted loose, boyish dresses with hemlines at the knee showing a shocking amount of leg. Serving hard liquor was against the law during that decade (Prohibition), leaving the only suppliers of liquor for the public in the hands of racketeers, bootleggers, and gangsters.

Automobiles had improved tremendously. Fast cars had become symbolic of this decade, along with the fast dance of the Charleston and the fast music of jazz.

The bubbly tempo and quick appeal to the emotions of jazz music grew from two earlier styles of music from the late 1800s—blues and ragtime. Ellington recognized that jazz "is a music with an African foundation which came out of an American environment."[2]

The blues developed from simple but powerful African-American folk music. Either sung a cappella or played with an instrumental, the blues performers deliberately flattened certain notes. These 'blue' notes mimicked the cry of a human voice showing both sorrow and resilience in the face of trouble in the words of the song.

Ragtime, on the other hand, combined aspects of both black and white musical traditions. Its ragged, syncopated pulses, caused by playing the melody slightly ahead of or behind the beat makes a bouncy, more joyful music than the blues.

The earliest known jazz bands were New Orleans brass bands playing at parades, dances, and funerals around the turn of the century, combining the soul and spirit of the blues with the rhythmic jolt of ragtime. At first called jass, it soon was known as jazz.[3]

The new musical idea of jazz was the concept of improvisation, or creating on-the-spot variations from the basic music. At first the New Orleans musicians improvised together, bouncing ideas off each other during performances. Compared to the slow, sedate music of that time, it surprised and sometimes shocked audiences. During the early 1920s, improvisations became the specialty of the "hot" soloist, moving to stand at the front of the band as he took off musically.

Ellington meshed the group jazz style with his own hot soloist, trumpeter Bubber Miley. He composed pieces that would blend the soloist with the orchestra yet give him places to really stand out. He did this by toning down the raw power of jazz and adding elegance and sophistication yet keeping the raw, primitive power and flavor of the music. He helped jazz go from being considered the vulgar, uncultured sounds of the underprivileged to "the music of the decade."[4]

Ellington always felt the term jazz was too restrictive. He insisted jazz could also be done as an opera, a ballad, a ballet, a musical, or even a religious concert, and he proceeded to prove it by writing such music during the rest of his life.[5] He told a New York reporter, "I am not playing jazz. I am trying to play the natural feelings of [the black] people. . . . Our music is always intended to be definitely and purely racial."[6]

In 1927, one of the top spots in Harlem, the Cotton Club, needed a new orchestra. However, the club wanted an eleven-piece orchestra, and Ellington only had eight. Ellington passed the word that he needed people, and arrived at the audition with the required number. The only problem was, he was two hours late. All the other groups had performed. That was no problem. The managing owner, Harry Block, was also two hours late. Since the only orchestra he heard was Ellington's, Block hired him on the spot to begin the first week in December.

No one would admit that the club was owned by gangsters. Ellington himself denied knowing any gangsters, at least to the police who asked him almost every week. Actually, he knew them all. Many hung out at both the Kentucky Club and the Cotton Club. Once when some small-time thugs tried to extort money out of Ellington, the famous gangster Al Capone passed the word that Duke Ellington was not to be bothered. He was never bothered again.

The Cotton Club was established as a nightspot for white customers only, posh and expensive, in the midst of black Harlem. Men wore top hats and fur-collared chesterfield coats. The heavily lipsticked women wore fancy, frilly dresses. It was a place for the jaded elite to explore, with just that little bit of danger from gangsters to add spice. It was one of the few places white people could see a view of black culture that was handsome, accomplished, gifted, and elegant.

Once up the stairs and inside the Cotton Club, patrons discovered that manners were strictly enforced. Although bootlegged whiskey was available, no loud drunkenness or even loud talking was allowed among the audience of five hundred to seven hundred, especially during the floor show. If a drunk persisted, the waiters politely asked him to quiet down or be thrown out by the bouncer. Since the bouncers were huge bruisers, often ex-boxers, they had no trouble removing rowdy people.

The floor show consisted of from sixteen to thirty tall, elegantly gowned or sometimes scantily clad chorus girls who danced, sang, and acted out sketches to music. They were required to be twenty-one years old, at least five feet eleven inches tall, and lightly colored—of a shade known as "high yaller."[7]

Eventually a few of the richer African Americans were allowed to enter. However, most of the people in the Harlem neighborhood were allowed in only to work as waiters, bus boys, dishwashers, cooks, or on the stage as entertainers.

Although music was Ellington's passion, it did not stop him from charming the women of all colors who crowded his dressing room backstage at the Cotton Club and throughout his musical career. His sister Ruth says, "It was shocking" how women threw themselves at him.[8]

Because he had such a vibrant personality, he got away with using lines of chat that would have sounded like false flattery from anyone else, such "I'm so jealous of your frock, . . . Because it's closer to you than I will ever be,"[9] or "Does your contract stipulate that you must be this pretty?"[10]

Ellington did not fit the image of either black or white band and orchestra conductors of the 1920s. Whereas most other conductors drew attention to themselves by flashy clothing and wildly waving batons, Ellington, in a white dinner jacket, conducted his group in a dignified manner with small gestures either standing near or sitting at the piano. He was the epitome of cool and sophistication.

During the floor show, Ellington's orchestra played show tunes and popular music written by other people. It was during the interludes that he was free to offer up his own compositions.

Ellington not only experimented with the music to create a sophisticated jazz sound, he also experimented with the stage show. He was the first to put the band behind a screen to create shadow pictures or silhouettes of the bandmembers as they performed.

Ellington expected his orchestra members to dress well. Sonny Greer's elegant appearance outshone even Ellington's. In addition, Greer bought a $3,000 drum set for this gig complete with timpani, chimes, and vibraphone. On the big bass drum, he put both his monogram and that of Duke Ellington. Almost every band in the world does it now, but he was the first.

In the late 1920s, people all over the country discovered the new music Duke Ellington's Orchestra was creating when CBS Radio began broadcasting a one-hour musical show live from the floor of the Cotton Club every evening. Radio was brand new. The first station began broadcasting in 1916, and the business grew by leaps and bounds. Television may have been thought of, but the logistics had not been worked out yet. Movies had just been invented, and the movie studios were thinking about making the jump from silent films to 'talkies.'

Just as every family wants a television set now, radio became the thing every family had to have then. More and more people bought radios and record players to bring music into their homes. Ellington's evening show soon became popular both nationally and internationally and helped create a demand for his records.

At first, Ellington's Washington relatives were startled

Duke Ellington sent this publicity shot to his father in Washington, D.C. Ellington expected his orchestra members to dress well, as he did.

to hear his music described as "jungle music" when they tuned in to the broadcasts. On the other hand, some white people, especially music critics, were appalled by the music's weird chording and tempos. Still, the general public loved it.[11]

Ellington's orchestra perfected its sound during the four-year engagement at the Cotton Club, from 1927 until 1931. Ellington fine-tuned the jazz technique, giving it a vibrant, urban edge and converting it from mere entertainment of the masses to an art form to be taken seriously.

At this point, he had gathered the core of the orchestra that would remain with him for many years. However, two major performers had to be replaced. Bubber Miley and Otto Hardwick had begun showing up late, drunk, or not at all.[12] They even missed recording sessions, which meant that pieces featuring Miley's trumpet solos could not be recorded. They missed performances when important people in the music business were in the audience, coming especially to hear Ellington's sound, featuring Miley.

Ellington was not good at firing anyone. He eventually worked out a technique of making life so unpleasant for a band member that he would quit. Without warning, Ellington would set the tempo at an impossible speed, then give the cue for the drunken performer to come forward and do his solo piece. The humiliation would either sober him up or make him decide to quit. Either way, the problem was solved.

In this way he got rid of Hardwick in 1928 and Miley in 1929.[13] He hired Charley "Cootie" Williams, a young, seventeen-year-old with a New Orleans jazz spirit and style. Ellington never instructed him about using the plunger mute and growling. He told Cootie to find his own way of doing what feels right. Tricky Sam Nanton took him aside and taught him the finer points of mute work. Williams, being a perfectionist, quickly grasped the concept and developed an even flashier style than Miley's.

He worked with Ellington's orchestra until November 1940. Williams rejoined Ellington in 1962 and remained his star soloist until his death.

Ellington was the first to use the human voice as an instrument in his orchestra in 1927. While his orchestra rehearsed the song "Creole Love Call" at the Cotton Club, singer Adelaide Hall, who was standing in the wings, began singing along. Ellington liked the effect of her vocalizing sound without words so well, he asked her to come to the recording studio the next day and repeat it with the orchestra.[14] It became a hit recording.

Irving Mills and Ellington signed an agreement in 1928 giving each other 45 percent of a joint corporation owning Ellington's compositions and other joint income. The remaining 10 percent was owned by Mills' lawyer.

Some members of the Duke Ellington Orchestra pose for a photo. Otto Hardwick left the orchestra in 1928. Shown here are (from left to right): Otto Hardwick, Harry Carney, Barney Priest, and Johnny Hodges.

This agreement gave Mills a personal interest in Ellington's success and gave Ellington some independent income from some of Mills' other investments.

It also gave Ellington almost total control over his orchestra. Since only Ellington dealt with the music publisher and promoter, if other band members did not like it, all they could do was quit. They could not discuss or overrule Ellington's decisions like they had done in Washington, D.C. This arrangement with Mills lasted until 1939.

In 1929, Edna and Duke agreed to separate permanently. They never legally divorced. Ellington continued to consider her his wife and supported her the rest of her life, providing her with a house in Washington and all her other needs.

Ellington's legal marriage to Edna kept the most predatory females away from him. Yet it did not stop him from developing short-term relationships with other women. It merely kept them from expecting Ellington to marry them. After he separated from his wife, he developed long-term relationships with two former Cotton Club show girls: Mildred Dixon in the 1930s and Beatrice (Evie) Ellis from the 1940s on. Although Dixon traveled with the orchestra on tour, Ellis was rarely seen in public with him. Ellington never married either woman, not even after his wife, Edna, died in 1966.

When Ellington moved from his wife to living with Dixon, and again when he moved in with Ellis, he took nothing from his previous life. He left all his furniture and clothing behind. Mercer had to decide on his own whether he wished to move with his father.

Life was grand. It seemed everyone had money. Everyone wanted to visit the Cotton Club. Ellington's records were selling well. No one expected the stock market to crash.

7

![decorative band]

ADORATION IN EUROPE/PREJUDICE AT HOME

![decorative band]

he Stock Market Crash of October 1929 stopped the flow of money. Many rich people suddenly found themselves poor and unable to afford nightly or weekly visits to nightclubs like the Cotton Club.

Although the Cotton Club lasted for another decade or so, they no longer offered long-term contracts. They began alternating Ellington and his orchestra with other bands in an attempt to attract customers. For a while, Ellington and his orchestra traveled with vaudeville acts.

Irving Mills still poured his energies into promoting

The Duke Ellington Orchestra at the Cotton Club preparing for a show in 1930. Notice the megaphone Sonny Greer (center) is holding. Before microphones were invented, singers with an orchestra used a megaphone to project their voices.

Ellington's orchestra. Every day he broke barriers. He not only got them into an Amos 'n' Andy movie called *Check and Double Check*, but he also managed to line up short feature films starring Duke Ellington and his Orchestra.

During the 1930s, he managed to get them into other films starring white actors, such as *Belle of the Nineties*, *Murder at the Vanities*, and *The Hit Parade*.

In *Murder at the Vanities*, the scene showing an eighteenth-century orchestra playing one of Franz Liszt's Hungarian rhapsodies dissolves into Duke Ellington's orchestra swinging with a jazz version of the same tune. This so offends a classical conductor that he mows them down with a machine gun.

All this time, Ellington was still as attached to his mother as she was to him. During his New York City success in the Roaring Twenties, he took the money he earned and showered her with gifts—long ropes of pearls, a fur coat, an extravagant car called a Pierce-Arrow limousine complete with a chauffeur to drive it. Whenever his mother protested, he would declare, "If you don't take these things, I won't work."[1]

Despite the distance in miles between them, they remained close. In fact, his mother seemed to develop asthma whenever he was not around. After Ellington broke up with his wife, Edna, he invited his mother and father to come live with him in New York City. They arrived in 1930, bringing his sister Ruth. Immediately, his mother's asthma vanished, never to reappear.

Ruth Ellington remembers that their mother was "happy to be caring and cooking for her son again, waiting each day for him to come through the door and shout, 'Mother, I'm home to dine!'"[2]

She would use that limousine to follow him from show to show when he was on tour and was his biggest

Duke Ellington always remained close to his family. Shown here are his favorite people: his mother, Daisy; his father, James; and his sister, Ruth.

fan. "After a couple of thousand people had stopped applauding," his sister remembers, "my mother was always *still* applauding."[3]

When Ellington decided to take the orchestra on tour across the United States, he enlarged the brass section to three trombonists and added a singer, Ivie Anderson. Throughout the years, other female singers toured with the band, but "Ivie Anderson was always considered the best, the one who most closely matched Ellington's unique sound."[4]

In 1932, "Creole Rhapsody" won an award as "best new work by an American composer."[5]

In many ways, Ellington was a typical artist. If something inspired him, it was all-important. If it did not, it did not exist. Money was in the second category for him. Deep in his soul, he knew money was necessary to pay the rent and buy food and clothing. However, it had nothing to do with creating music and therefore, "rather than attaching importance to it, he dismissed it, and this attitude was reflected throughout his life."[6]

Ellington once said, "I want to create the music of the American Negro."[7] His courteous reply to a man who wrote him that he should take his jungle music and go back to Africa as soon as possible was that, unfortunately, it was impossible for him to do that because the blood of the "American Negro" had become so mixed over the years with that of the letter writer that Ellington might not be accepted in Africa. He would consider going to Europe, though. "There we are accepted."[8]

Accepted they were. Ellington, his orchestra, and his jazz music was adored in Europe long before they were accepted by the majority of Americans.

In 1933, Mills arranged a tour of Europe for the band, including a date at the London Palladium, one of the most prestigious variety theaters in the world. Ellington's records had been promoted heavily in Europe to the extent that Ellington discovered his music more popular there than at home.

There was one small problem. Ellington was afraid to travel by boat. His mother had scared him to death by repeatedly telling him how, when she was pregnant with Ellington, she had been on a ferryboat that sank.[9] Not only that, but when he had been a young boy, he had read the newspaper accounts of the sinking of the *Titanic*.

The captain of the ship taking them to Europe tried to reassure him that the ship was being steered by an automatic pilot. Ellington mumbled something about not understanding how an automatic pilot can see an iceberg. He stayed up the entire night watching for icebergs. The next night he tried to convince some of his bandmembers to come help him watch, but the few who joined him soon fell asleep.

When they arrived in Europe, they found themselves

welcomed by fans and interviewed by music critics who seemed to understand jazz.

After the performance at the Palladium, Lord Beaverbrook, a newspaper tycoon, hosted a party for Ellington and his orchestra members. Among the English royalty attending were Prince George (who later became King of England), the Duke of Kent, and the Prince of Wales.

While Duke Ellington and Prince George played four hand duets on the piano, the Prince of Wales sat at Sonny Greer's side, taking a turn on the drums. By the end of the evening, the prince was calling the drummer Sonny, and Greer was calling the prince "The Wale." "The Wale" introduced Ellington to others as "The Duke of Hot."[10]

From then on, Ellington's concerts were sold out all over England. The Prince of Wales followed them to several venues, even buying cheap tickets at Liverpool and sitting in the back of the audience. When he was recognized, the working class audience cheered both for the orchestra and for the prince.

The tour continued through Holland and on to Paris, receiving critical acclaim everywhere.

Immediately after this success, in the fall of 1933, Ellington toured the American South. What a difference this was. Only once had they run into racial prejudice in England. One major hotel had accepted Ellington but refused to let the orchestra members stay, sending them to the low-rent district of London. However, prejudice was the norm in the American South.

For years, Irving Mills had worked to make certain that Ellington and his orchestra were treated with the consideration and dignity due a fine artist, no matter the color of his skin. He succeeded in insuring that they were given as much respect as African-American artists were given in that segregated time.

While Ellington was growing up, there was "never any talk about red people, brown people, black people, or yellow people, or about differences that existed between them. . . . I was quite grown up when I first heard about all that."[11]

Ellington remembered being taught in eighth grade that every African American would find himself or herself in the spotlight:

> . . . for every time people saw a Negro they would go into a reappraisal of the [whole] race. She taught us that proper speech and good manners were our first obligations, because, as representatives of the Negro race we were to command respect for our people. . . . They had pride there, the greatest race pride. . . .[12]

As a result, Ellington refused to knuckle under to blatant racism. However, he did not try to force himself through every door in society. He kept his poise, dignity, and self-confidence and simply worked around the problem.

The laws in the American South declared that

separate hotels and restaurants for whites and blacks were legal. This made it difficult for the orchestra members to give a concert when they arrived in a town. They had to find a hotel (if there was one) in the African-American section of town to park their bags. They then would rush to the concert venue or dance hall, which was usually in the white neighborhood, for their rehearsal and sound check. Then they had to decide whether there was enough time to rush back to the African-American section of town to find a place to eat before the performance.

Ellington's solution to the whole problem was to hire two private Pullman cars (sleeping train cars) for himself and his band members, plus a seventy-foot baggage car. On the sides, a sign was posted advertising his orchestra—DUKE ELLINGTON.

He instructed Mills to only schedule concerts in towns accessible by train. That way they lived in comfortable isolation in the train yards. With the Pullman hooked up to electricity, water, and sanitation facilities, they were pampered and well fed by the African-American train cooks and waiters. As Ellington tactfully explained, this "avoided any unnecessary contact with *objectionable* people."[13]

Harry Carney remembers:

The drag was [the concert audience would] be screaming and applauding and afterward you'd have to go back across the tracks. . . . In Europe we were royalty;

in Texas, we were back in the colored section. It was some adjustment, but we were young and could take it.[14]

Although the European music critics praised Ellington's jazz compositions, the racial prejudice of the American music critics showed when most of them refused to even recognize jazz as a respectable art form.

A white police officer stopped Ellington one day just to tell him how much he liked Ellington's music. "If you were white, you'd be a great composer."[15] Although the police officer sincerely meant it as a compliment, it was a backhanded one.

After that, Ellington attempted to only accept gigs where they were respected, avoiding those parts of the country where they would be badly treated.

Although it is more common today for music stars to hire their own private buses or planes for themselves and the people who travel with them, the Ellington orchestra was the only group at that time traveling in their own private train car.

Even with the comfort of their own space to go back to each night, constantly traveling to one-night gigs for six or more months of the year wore people out. (Rock musicians on tour today usually perform for two months, then take a month or two off to recover.) Traveling from town to town became boring. When they arrived in town, it was rush, rush, rush, perform the concert, rush back to the train, and travel overnight to the next stop.

They could only sleep so much time away. They filled the remaining travel hours with endless rounds of card games. Ivie Anderson became the group's best stud poker player.

Practical jokes helped keep their dull lives interesting. There could be nothing worse than to pull on a uniform, go onstage to perform, then discover someone had sprinkled itching powder in the uniform. The victim could not run offstage. He knew he should not scratch in front of the audience. He could not tear the uniform off in front of hundreds of people.

Trumpet player Freddy Jenkins had a habit of licking his mouthpiece before beginning to blow his trumpet. Hardwick smeared the mouthpiece with essence of hot peppers.

No one ever confessed to being the person who set off the stink bomb in the middle of a concert that made life miserable for the soloist performing in the path of the cloud of stink.

As long as the practical jokes remained within the orchestra, Ellington pretended not to notice them. He understood that the jokes helped diffuse tension and helped the whole group relax.

Most of the musicians stuck with the job despite the boredom. After all, there was a depression out there, and this job paid better than most other jobs an African American could get. If they reached their limit and needed time off, they just quit.

Ellington found himself the butt of a joke in Tacoma, Washington. He was a sound sleeper. It was the responsibility of the road manager to awaken him and make sure Ellington got to the concert venue in plenty of time. The road manager got so frustrated at being unable to awaken Ellington that he instructed that Ellington's Pullman be shunted off onto a siding five miles from the station. When Ellington finally awoke, he had to walk all the way back.

Another time Ellington stumbled from his sleeping car still half asleep. He joined a line of men climbing onto a bus and found himself sitting with criminals on their way to San Quentin Prison. The road manager noticed just in time. He chased the bus with a borrowed car. It was difficult to convince the bus driver that Ellington was a famous musical conductor, not a criminal.

Although his men grew exhausted during a tour, Ellington used the traveling time to absorb inspiration and compose music. In the early days, he socialized with his musicians. Once when they traveled in a train car with no electric lights, his men held matches to illuminate the paper on which he scribbled his latest composition. Later on he arranged for a separate car for himself to give him more time alone for writing music.

Ellington would vary the tours with short gigs at nightclubs like the still-open Cotton Club or occasional radio or movie work.

The group was still recording. The Ellington hits in the 1930s included "Sophisticated Lady," "Mood Indigo," "Drop Me off in Harlem," "It Don't Mean a Thing If It Ain't Got That Swing," "Solitude," and the exotic sounding "Caravan."

Daisy Ellington developed cancer and died in 1935. Duke stayed by her bedside for three days as she died. Her death tipped Ellington into a deep depression.[16] He stopped composing music. "He sat around the house and wept for days at a time." Mercer Ellington explained, "He lost his ambition because he had lost the person he most liked to please."[17]

Eventually he commemorated her life with a piece called "Reminiscing in Tempo," which attempted to express both his grief at his mother's death and his remembrance of all the good times they had together. This unusual tone poem took up both sides of two 78 rpm records.

For many years afterward, he found it extremely difficult to face the anniversary of her death. He tried to drown his grief every year on that date with a bout of heavy drinking.

He refused to ever wear anything brown because he had been wearing it the day his mother died. He preferred blue, because his mother had always dressed him in blue on Sundays. As for the color green, he loathed it. "It reminded him of grass. He thought grass unnatural: it reminded him of graves."[18] It especially reminded him of his parent's graves. His father did not survive his wife very long. He died in 1937.

During the 1930s, teens were looking for danceable music, which was not always possible with jazz. In the mid-1920s, Fletcher Henderson's band, featuring Louis Armstrong, had begun a variation of jazz with a highly danceable rhythm called "swing." It was picked up and made famous in the 1930s by a white clarinetist named Benny Goodman and his band. This was the beginning of the Big Band sound.

Ellington refused to limit himself to whatever the current popular sound was. He continued to play his old hits and kept composing new ones—ballads and experimental music.

Promoters started a trend of featuring several bands together in the same venue, calling it a "Battle of the Bands," where the dancers voted for the best band. In the late 1930s, Ellington entered the Savoy Ballroom in New York City to battle a band considered the best swing band in Harlem, Chick Webb's wild group. Webb's band did not have a chance. Ellington's orchestra worked the crowd into a dancing fury. Webb's trombonist, Sandy Williams, reported, "They outswung us, they out everythinged us."[19]

Ellington was still the Duke of Hot.

8

THE WAR YEARS

he year 1939 was a busy year in Ellington's life. That was the year when Ellington separated from his agent Irving Mills. To achieve this, Ellington traded his own monetary interest in the Cab Calloway Band for Mills' shares in Ellington's band. He was not without an agent for long. He was snapped up by the huge William Morris agency.

The second major change happened when Billy Strayhorn, a young, classically trained composer, attended an Ellington concert where Duke played a moving free adaptation of Franz Liszt's "Hungarian Rhapsody" called "Ebony Rhapsody."

"I was lost [in the beautiful music],"[1] Billy Strayhorn said. From that point on, his interest took a sharp turn away from classical music to jazz. He joined Ellington a year later, never leaving until his death in 1967.

Ellington hired Strayhorn as a lyricist but discovered he had a brilliant feel for arranging and writing music. They became musical collaborators. Ellington put him to work arranging music, taking the lead line Ellington produced and writing out the parts for the various instruments. By doing this tedious work, Strayhorn gave Ellington more time to compose, conduct, and perform.

From then on, every piece Ellington wrote passed through Strayhorn's hands for polishing. Anything Strayhorn composed independently, Ellington also worked on, making certain it had the Ellington style. They talked over the music and tossed it back and forth, each adding his own interpretation to it.

Both men's work benefited from this collaboration to the point where neither one could point out just which parts were created by one or the other. Ellington's improvisational, emotional music merged with Strayhorn's smoother, more structured, classically based and polished creations into an improved, blended, satisfying whole. Both men wrote pieces with the individual members of the orchestra in mind—showing off their greatest talents.

Strayhorn remained in Ellington's shadow. He sometimes traveled as a performer with the orchestra, other times remaining in New York City, composing and arranging, keeping in touch with Ellington during his tours by telephone and telegraph. It was as if they both were on the same musical wavelength. They could produce almost identical musical themes even when on opposite coasts of the country.

He also served as Ellington's ears outside the orchestra, keeping Ellington in touch with the changes in the music world. He helped keep Ellington's work up-to-date in appeal.

One of the first works attributed to Strayhorn became the new theme song for Ellington's orchestra—"Take the 'A' Train." Strayhorn claimed he merely was writing subway directions to get a New Yorker to Harlem.

Strayhorn was twenty-three when he joined the forty-year-old Ellington. They developed a close father/son relationship. The small, elegant, but physically weak Strayhorn looked up to the tall, elegant, physically imposing and sophisticated Ellington who was always every inch "the Duke." The members of the orchestra affectionately called the lovable little man either "Strays" or "Swee' Pea."[2]

The third adventure of 1939 concerned a planned

tour of Europe. Europe in 1939 was feeling the rumblings of World War II. Hitler's daily broadcasts warned against the inferior races such as *die Swartze* (the blacks) *und die Juden* (and the Jews). Jazz was banned in Germany for being music from a lesser race.

Nevertheless, Ellington was committed to taking his group on tour in Europe. They had a few close calls. At one point, their tour train was scheduled to cut through Germany on its way to Denmark. An unexpected layover in Hamburg, Germany, however, caused a ". . . painful six hours as 20 some odd black people waited around for the next train, fearing from second to second that the worst would suddenly happen." However, Ellington commented later that they were "strangely ignored."[3]

Again the Duke Ellington Orchestra was warmly welcomed by audiences. The Grand Hotel in Stockholm, Sweden, organized a huge birthday party for Ellington with all-day festivities in his honor.

Because of the talk of war, the group cut the tour short, not returning to Europe until after peace came in the late 1940s.

Ellington's music remained popular in the United States. Many people regard 1940 as a high point in his career.[4]

In 1941, during a stint in Hollywood, Ellington joined with a group of Hollywood writers, including the poet and novelist Langston Hughes, to write the stage play *Jump for Joy*. Another musician, Sid Kuller, remembers "Duke serenely composing the score between gigs on a portable keyboard at a 'Negroes only' hotel, while roaches and rats scurried about."[5]

The show drew death threats from the Ku Klux Klan for portraying African Americans in nonstereotypical roles. It called for a huge cast. Despite the standing room only audience response, it only ran for three months. When the United States entered World War II, most stage shows, including this one, closed down as their cast members were drafted into the armed services.

In 1943, his orchestra was the first African-American group to play in the prestigious New York City venue of Carnegie Hall. He premiered his first long piece, "Black, Brown, and Beige." It was an attempt to merge classical music with African-American spirituals and jazz, tracing the African-American struggle from slavery to modern days. It established him as an American composer of serious music. Although "Black, Brown, and Beige" was not critically well received, the audience loved it.

At these concerts, Ellington occasionally performed several compositions written by his son, Mercer, now a musician in his own right and leader of a band of his own. Mercer said the reason he wanted to enter the music world is that when he was a young boy in 1927 he heard the Duke Ellington Orchestra

Duke Ellington collaborated with Hollywood writers to write the stage play *Jump for Joy*. Shown here is the cover of the play's sheet music.

perform and "I saw they were having so much fun that I had to be a part of it."[6]

During the war, Ellington's group found itself in financial trouble. No records were being cut because of a dispute between the musician's union and the record companies. Gas was rationed, and train travel limited. The group remained in the New York City area playing club dates and dance halls.

Finally, in 1943, when Ellington had spent his last savings to pay his bandmembers' salaries, he approached his agent, William Morris, for a loan of at least $500 to tide them over. When he entered the office, the agent's secretary handed him a letter. Inside was a royalty check from a popular band who had recorded one of his songs. At first he thought the check was made out for $2,250.00. That would be a nice amount to keep him and his orchestra going. Then he double-checked, wondering if he had misread it. Yes, he had. The check was made out for $22,500.00! The group who had recorded it remained well known for several more decades—The Ink Spots.[7]

The Duke Ellington Orchestra's last appearance together as an orchestra in film was in 1943 in *Cabin in the Sky*, which also featured blues singers Lena Horne and Ethel Waters, jazz trumpet great Louis Armstrong, and fellow jazz conductor Cabell "Cab" Calloway and his band. Calloway's band had been Ellington's backup band at the Cotton Club.

Several members of Ellington's orchestra left during World War II. Shown here are the members of the Duke Ellington Orchestra in 1944. Ellington himself is sitting at the piano.

Several members of Ellington's orchestra left during World War II. Cootie Williams decided to join Benny Goodman's band. At that time, it was one of the top bands in the country. When Ellington learned of it, he helped his star trumpet player negotiate a good contract, making certain Williams got paid what he deserved. (Twenty-two years later, Williams rejoined Ellington.) The idea that Williams would leave Ellington's orchestra so shocked the music world that Raymond Scott, another bandleader, wrote and recorded a song called "When Cootie Left the Duke."[8]

9

JAZZ BECOMES MAINSTREAM

hen World War II was over and the recording dispute settled, the big bands found themselves in trouble. The now popular bebop sound featured smaller groups who used a more improvisational style, less shading of sound, and more power playing. In addition, a group of white Dixieland jazz bands sprang up featuring smaller brass sections than Ellington used.

Ellington found himself trying to hold the middle ground. His group was too large to be bebop and too different from Dixieland. Other big bands folded—Benny

Goodman, Tommy Dorsey, Benny Carter, Woody Herman, and Count Basie.

Ellington's next stage show, *Beggar's Holiday*, opened at the Broadway Theater in New York City in 1946. Selecting the cast by ability, not race, resulted in a love interest between a white actor and a black actress, both playing British characters. This, and the fact that the show was just too long, resulted in the show being panned by the critics and ignored by the audiences.

Ellington always felt that "by celebrating African-American culture through music in a positive manner, thereby instilling a sense of pride in their heritage, it could do more good in the long run than grabbing a rifle and waving it around making a speech."[1]

In the early 1950s, when Ellington found it difficult to find bookings, he supported himself and his musicians by contracts for recordings of his old compositions and the royalty income. Only retrospectives of his older works were still in demand, so that was what they recorded. Using the royalties to pay them insured the band was always on hand, instantly available for rehearsing a new piece a few hours after it was written.

Strayhorn shared Ellington's mad desire to hear a new piece of music performed as soon as possible. Strayhorn once said, "Ellington plays the piano, but his real instrument is the band."[2] Ellington confessed he did it because "I give the musicians the money and I get the kicks."[3]

Their lowest point seemed to be in 1955 when they were booked at the Aquacades. It was the worst gig they had ever had.

That year Ellington alone was invited to be the master of ceremonies at the Newport American Jazz Festival in Rhode Island.

When the Duke Ellington Orchestra was invited to participate as a group in the 1956 Newport American Jazz Festival, it was as a tribute to a band that used to be good.

Although they were scheduled to be the last act on one of the very last nights, a place reserved for unimportant groups, they turned it into a triumph. Their performance blew the crowd away. The recording became a top seller for Columbia Records for many, many years.

The *Time* magazine cover story, interviewed and photographed the previous April to celebrate Ellington's twenty-five years in the music business, came out just after the Newport Jazz Festival. This further helped put Ellington's jazz back on top.

The American people began to recognize his brilliance as a composer and arranger. Students of music began tracing his development and rediscovered the excellence of the golden years of his 1938 to

1942 orchestra, considered one of the best groups of musicians he had ever gathered.

In 1957 he composed and performed "Such Sweet Thunder" for the Shakespearean festival at Stratford, Ontario, Canada. Joachim Berendt, in his book *Die Grosse Jazzbuch* (The Big Jazz Book) describes this piece as the first of a string of new masterpieces. He says, "With its spirited glosses . . . and caricatures of great Shakespearean characters, it is one of the most beautiful of the larger Ellington works."[4]

Ellington's short comic opera, *A Drum Is a Woman*, was performed on television—in color, a new development at that time. It was a history of jazz from its African roots to the present told through music and dance.

In 1958 he took his group to England where they performed for Queen Elizabeth II and her sister, Princess Margaret. Ellington wrote and performed a special suite called *Princess Blue*. When he met the queen afterward, he promised her that he would compose something just for her.

Later, when he saw his first view of the Northern Lights, he and Strayhorn composed a piece of music expressing his awe at the sight. He recorded this, along with several other pieces, as *The Queen's Suite*. He had one copy made and sent to Queen Elizabeth II as a private gift from a duke to a queen. He refused to allow it to be released to the public. Mercer

In 1958, Duke Ellington performed a special suite for Queen Elizabeth II, of England. Here, Ellington is shown with the queen.

Ellington issued the beautiful, majestic suite two years after his father's death.

In 1959, Ellington won three Grammy awards (awards from the music association) for his first complete major film score—*Anatomy of a Murder*, directed by Otto Preminger and starring James Stewart. In that film, he also played piano in one scene. Six years later he worked with Frank Sinatra on *Assault on a Queen*. He composed his last movie score for *Change of Mind* in 1969.

In 1963, his son Mercer disbanded his own band and began managing his father's orchestra. Duke Ellington remembered how disastrous it had been for Cab Calloway when Calloway's sister's band started making a big name for itself. There should not be two Ellingtons in the business. By getting Mercer both as manager and trumpet player, he kept all the family talent working for the same orchestra.

Duke Ellington hated making decisions. He preferred peace and tranquility and creating music.[5] As manager, Mercer used his college training in accounting to straighten out his father's finances. He had to assert his authority over these men, many of whom had taken care of him when he was a child and who still saw him as a child. But if a band member needed to be disciplined and his father could not face up to it, Mercer had to become the enforcer.

As a result, Mercer Ellington had many conflicts

Anatomy of a Murder was Ellington's first film score in twenty-five years. He is shown here with film director Otto Preminger and arranger Billy Strayhorn.

with the musicians and with Duke Ellington himself. However, because Mercer had run his own ten-piece band, he had become enough of a success to be self-confident when he began managing his father's group. Mercer recalled:

> One day I had nerve enough to advise him how lucky he was to have me for a son. I said, "You know, I'm the only *NO* man you've got. I'm the one who'll tell you what is wrong." Everyone else was admiring him so much. But, if he wrote something and it didn't come off well, I would tell him.[6]

On the road, Mercer Ellington rode with the musicians, not with his father.

During the 1960s, the United States State Department sent Ellington and his orchestra around the world on goodwill tours—to the Near East in 1963, the Orient in 1964, Africa in 1966, South and Central America in 1968, Eastern Europe in 1969, and the Soviet Union in 1971. The bandmembers were able to catch some sleep between the plane's landings and performing the concerts. But Duke Ellington, older than any of them, had to go straight from the plane to meeting and greeting officials and interviews with radio and television.

Ellington loved to dress elegantly with well-tailored suits, cashmere sweaters, and handmade shoes and slippers in public, gorgeous dressing gowns in private. It is said that he bought a new suit every week, sometimes wearing eight of them a day. He refused to wear a shirt after a button had fallen off, therefore he owned hundreds of shirts.

He had odd eating habits. Being his own boss, he could eat his dessert first, and he did, enjoying his pie with whipped cream and a touch of syrup dotted with maraschino cherries. He said that "it made a meal set better."[7] He dumped multiple packets of sugar into the endless Coca-Colas he drank late at night to give him energy. He could eat three quarts of ice cream at a time. Eventually the rich food he ate on tours

During the 1960s, the United States State Department sent Ellington and his orchestra around the world on goodwill tours. Here, Ellington tries to read an article about his show in an Italian magazine.

thickened his girth so much that his doctor insisted he lose twenty-two pounds—which he did.

Many superstitions ruled his life. He believed that drafts caused colds and sickness. To prove it, he said it once took him weeks to recover from a bout of fresh air poisoning contracted in Virginia Beach. The other reason he made certain all the windows in his house or motel room were shut was a fear of lightning leaping through an open window.

He thought the number thirteen was his lucky number. This was based on the fact that many good things did happen to him on Friday the thirteenth.

Ellington also loved the telephone. He would make long-distance calls at all hours of the night.

He was constantly in touch with his personal physician and close friend, Arthur Logan. Dr. Logan indulged Ellington's hypochondria by supplying a doctor's bag to the musician before each tour. The bag contained vitamin pills and drugs, except for aspirin, for every possible sickness. Ellington did not think much of aspirin.

Ellington intended to live as long as possible. When he was younger, he had indulged himself, but when he saw his friends dying young from the results of heavy drinking and other excesses, he decided to change his ways. He began taking care of his body with vitamins, rest, and proper diet, getting his body in shape and keeping it that way. He did not stop smoking, though.

Like many performers, his days and nights were reversed from that of normal people. After a concert, on his way to the next gig or in his hotel room, he would practice on his portable keyboard or compose new music. He made sure to get to bed around 9:00 A.M. When he awakened about 2:00 or 3:00 P.M., he would spend the next few hours flat on his back, making phone calls or discussing business with people who came to his room. He moved as little as possible, conserving his strength and energy.

His creativity even extended to designing comfortable robes and slippers for himself to wear before and after performances. Some days he could not bear to get out of his comfortable velvet slippers and even wore them onstage.

When Mercer's hair became gray before his father's did, Ellington jokingly referred to Mercer as his father, not the other way around. The closer Ellington got to old age, the less he liked the idea. It was a family trait. His father had been the same way. Ellington even refused to talk to a middle-aged woman who approached him one day. He would not acknowledge that this graying woman was the same person he had dated many years ago when she was young and attractive.

On the other hand, when he met a seventy-year-old

Ellington signed autographs in the comfort of his dressing gown. He designed his own dressing gowns and velvet slippers.

woman after a show in the early 1970s, he sat and talked with her for an hour, ignoring his other responsibilities. They corresponded until his death. His agent says he could captivate anyone with his charm and could create conversation from nothing.

He largely ignored the fact that his young, matinee idol, impossibly handsome self had also aged. His " . . . heavy pouches under his deep-lidded eyes were his battle scars from a lifetime of nocturnal composition and dissipation."[8] He jokingly claimed the bags under his weary eyes represented "an accumulation of virtue."[9] His voice remained deep, his wit remained sharp, his smile still shone at more than two hundred watts, and he continued to dress like a prince (or a duke).

It seemed he would never bow to old age and stop touring.

10

Honors and Afterward

uring his lifetime, Duke Ellington saw more of the inside of the White House than his father had. However, unlike his father, Duke Ellington went as a performer and a guest.

In the late 1940s, President Harry Truman invited Ellington to the White House. After the reception, Truman invited Ellington into his study where they showed off for each other on the President's piano, traded stories, and generally acted like "a couple of cats in a billiard parlor."[1]

In the 1950s, Ellington performed for President Dwight Eisenhower. The President asked if he were planning to play "Mood Indigo." Ellington assured him he would, and he did—four times during the evening.

In the 1960s, Ellington was invited to the White House seven times by President Lyndon Johnson— only twice as an entertainer. The other five times he was invited as a guest. Ellington's most emotional visit to the White House was when he was invited by President Richard Nixon in 1969.

President Nixon invited Ellington to celebrate his seventieth birthday at the White House with a dinner, a concert, and a reception. The President's staff worked hard to provide a guest list of friends, relatives, and political guests from both sides of the government. They conferred with Ellington as to whom he would prefer to have invited. The list became a summary of all the friends Ellington had made over the years.

The Nixon family mingled with the Ellington family: his sister Ruth (who wore a fashionable blond wig for the occasion), and his son, Mercer, together with Mercer's wife and their three children. Representing his peers in the music world were band leaders Benny Goodman, Count Basie, Cab Calloway, Dave Brubeck, and Dizzy Gillespie.

A good portion of his orchestra attended, as did his long-time doctor and friend, Arthur Logan. The remaining guests included Vice President Spiro Agnew, university presidents, film director Otto

President Nixon invited Ellington to the White House to celebrate Ellington's seventieth birthday. Shown are (from left to right): President Nixon, Pat Nixon, Ruth Ellington (in a blond wig), and Ellington, himself.

Preminger, publishers, ministers, lawyers, friends from other countries, and jazz musicians—white, Hispanic American, and African American.

They were all eager to be on hand to see the President of the United States honor Duke Ellington with the nation's highest civilian honor, the Presidential Medal of Freedom, for his lifetime contribution to music.

In the receiving line, the President noticed Ellington kissing everyone four times—twice on each side of the face. When he asked why, Ellington replied, with a twinkle in his eye, "One for each cheek, Mr. President."[2] After the President presented Ellington with the Medal of Freedom, Ellington and President Nixon exchanged knowing glances and smiles as Ellington kissed the President four times.

Ellington was his usual charming self with the women present, gracious to all and subservient to none. At one point he teased First Lady Pat Nixon this way:

"Mrs. Nixon, have you heard of the White House Ordinance?"

"White House Ordinance?" she said, perplexed.

"Yes. There is a law that no First Lady can be prettier than a certain degree, and you are exceeding the legal limit."[3]

Mrs. Nixon chuckled at the flattery. She had heard about his reputation of tossing exaggerated statements to women.

The party lasted past midnight and included a rendition of "Happy Birthday" pounded on the piano by President Nixon. Ellington was so happy he declared, "There is no place I would rather be tonight except in my mother's arms."[4]

Afterward, Ellington stopped by his hotel room, not to sleep, but simply to change out of his tuxedo, grab his suitcase, and hop a plane to Oklahoma. The next evening he was just as gracious to the midwesterners in Oklahoma City as he had been to the politically important guests at the White House.

During the rest of his life, many awards rolled in. Other countries awarded him their highest medals of honor. The countries of Chad and Togo issued commemorative postage stamps in his honor. (Long after his death, in 1986, the United States also issued a commemorative postage stamp.)

Seventeen universities awarded him honorary doctorates. His hometown of Washington, D.C., honored him by establishing the Duke Ellington School of the Arts, a senior high school specializing in music, dance, and the fine arts.

The Duke Ellington Collection at the Smithsonian Institute in Washington, D.C., contains more than three hundred of his awards.

During the 1960s, the beat of rock and roll became stronger in the music world. Ellington decided he was not going to follow this variation of rhythm and blues. It was out of character for him. He was a serious composer of jazz, and ". . . he didn't particularly care what anyone thought about his music, so long as he liked it personally."[5]

When Billy Strayhorn died in May of 1967, Otto "Toby" Hardwick reflected on their relationship, "Strayhorn's death was the one thing I know of that really touched Duke. . . . Neither money nor business was an issue between them, ever."[6]

The legacy of Duke Ellington lives on today. Shown is a living tribute to Ellington—the Duke Ellington School of the Arts in Washington, D.C., just a few miles from his old neighborhood.

After Strayhorn died, Ellington turned to a new kind of composition—the three *Sacred Concerts*. These concerts began when an Episcopalian priest asked him to perform at the Grace Cathedral in San Francisco. Instead of just performing a medley of his hits, Ellington decided to create something new. In the nave of the church, Ellington's orchestra played, backed by a church choir while dancers moved in the foreground.

He was very particular about how these *Sacred*

Concerts were performed, more so than usual. He took great care polishing the music and the staging. "You can jive with secular music, but you can't jive with the Almighty."[7] Jazz had come a long way—from the morally suspect nightclubs to the interior of a place of worship.

The *First Sacred Concert* premiered in September of 1965 in San Francisco. The *Second Sacred Concert* initially was performed at one of the largest churches in the world, seating over two thousand people—the Cathedral Church of St. John the Divine in New York City. This was so successful that requests for performances of it came from all over the world. Ellington performed it over fifty times.

The *Third Sacred Concert* was scheduled to be performed in Westminster Abbey in London in 1973. However, in 1972, X rays discovered that the illness the heavy-smoking Ellington had been complaining of for so long was lung cancer. He went ahead with the *Sacred Concert* performance anyway, taking time out to rest during rehearsal and the concert itself. This was followed by a short tour of Europe and several spots in Africa.

Mercer Ellington explained, "He just refused to admit that he was sick. . . . there wasn't much [medically] that could have been done for him either, so as long as he was capable of leading the band, he did."[8]

"The music kept him going," his granddaughter

A rehearsal takes place for one of Ellington's three *Sacred Concerts*. Fitting all the performers into the front of a church made for crowded conditions.

Mercedes Ellington has recalled. "This is what made him go through all the pain, the suffering of the last part of the sickness, of being out on the road. . . . It was something he had to do, every day."[9]

Finally in 1974, Ellington had to admit that he could no longer tour with his orchestra. He checked into a New York City hospital.

Every day friends, relatives, and members of his orchestra came to visit. He felt an urgent need to continue working. "I have so much to do, so much more I have to do."[10]

He refused to stop composing. His son set up his electric piano in the room. Ellington continued to work on the comic opera *Queenie Pie* and put the final touches on "The Three Black Kings," which was later used by the Alvin Ailey Dance Troupe. He did most of the final editing on the recording of the *Third Sacred Concert* held at Westminster Abbey. He toyed with other musical ideas.

At last, on May 25, 1974, he succumbed to pneumonia. He was seventy-five years old.

Two of his orchestra members also died that week and the three of them, Duke Ellington, Paul Gonsalves (of Newport fame), and Tyree Glenn (who first joined the band in 1947) were laid out together in the same funeral home. Evie Ellis was also hospitalized at that time and died soon after.

His funeral at the New York City Cathedral of St. John the Divine on May 27 was attended by thousands, many remaining outside, unable to get in. Many businesses all over the country, but especially in Harlem, closed for mourning. Radio stations played his music.

During the eulogies at the funeral service, jazz critic Ralph Gleason declared that Duke Ellington was "the greatest composer this American society has produced."[11] Stanley Dance gave a moving oration proclaiming that Ellington "was loved throughout the whole world. . . ."[12]

After his father's death, Mercer Ellington led the Duke Ellington Orchestra until his own death in 1996. Mercer Ellington is shown here in June 1995.

The Duke Ellington Orchestra continued to go strong under the baton of Mercer Ellington, until Mercer's own death in 1996. In fact, the day after his father's funeral, Mercer took the Duke Ellington Orchestra to Bermuda for a concert, because his father had committed the orchestra to this gig, with or without the maestro.

Mercer explained:

There's a reason the band is called the Duke Ellington Orchestra. We feel it is a family enterprise, much like

Macy's department store or Lincoln motor cars, and that as it goes through the generations, which we hope it will, the band will be out there, artistically and creatively. Duke Ellington's work as a composer will go from father to son, or from father to daughter.[13]

After Mercer's death in February 1996, his daughter Mercedes, who had conducted the Duke Ellington Orchestra many times before, carried on leading the group. Mercer's youngest son, Paul, often travels with the orchestra and is also likely to work with the band.

Duke Ellington's music is still available—not only recordings by him, but by other artists playing his music.

A recent development in technology has enabled his friend, singer Cleo Laine, to sing with Ellington and his orchestra. Ellington had asked Laine to do this while he was alive, but their schedules never coincided. She named the completed recording after one of her favorite Ellington songs—"Solitude."

Even a rock and roll group has used Ellington tunes. The rock group Chicago, which has a strong horn section as well as guitars, issued an album in 1995 called *Night and Day*. It is a tribute to the big band sound and fully one-third of the songs are Ellington's. They had met Ellington when they were invited to participate in a television special honoring Duke Ellington just before his death. When they thanked Ellington, he replied, "It is I who am honored, because you are the next Duke Ellingtons."[14]

Ellington had invented a new type of music. He

Many people and organizations honored Duke Ellington after his death. Here, the cast of one of the many medallions struck to honor Duke Ellington is shown.

had an " . . . insatiable need to break old rules, write new ones, break new ground, and to create and innovate."[15] He combined European harmony, the eight- and twelve-bar forms from the blues, and the thirty-two-bar form from popular American songs.

He did not like to call his music jazz. He preferred to call it American music, or Negro Music, or the music of his people. He did not limit himself to one style of music but tried various styles.

He refused to be classified by race or creed. The 1992 PBS documentary *Duke Ellington: Reminiscing in*

Tempo quotes him responding to a question about his people with, "My people? Now, which of my people? You know, I'm in several groups . . . the piano players, the listeners, those who aspire to be dilettantes . . . those who appreciate [the wine] Beaujolais."[16]

The highest praise Ellington could have for a person's performance was that a person was "beyond category," that he or she could never be classified as one thing or another but was superior in many things. Indeed, in the world of music, Ellington himself proved to be beyond any category ever invented.

CHRONOLOGY

1889—Edward Kennedy (Duke) Ellington is born in Washington, D.C., on April 29.

1914—Is inspired by the technique of pianist Harvey Brooks.

1915—Composes his first song, "The Soda Fountain Rag."

1917—Wins scholarship to Pratt Institute of Applied Art; decides to concentrate on being a musician instead.

1918—Forms his own band, manages others, and runs the business out of his sign painting shop; marries Edna Thompson.

1919—Meets Sonny Greer; son Mercer Ellington is born.

1923—Takes his band to New York City and becomes a success at the Kentucky Club.

1926—Composes "East St. Louis Toodle-Oo," his earliest important recording, which becomes the theme song of his orchestra; growling trumpets and "jungle sound" are invented; Irving Mills becomes his agent.

1927—His orchestra is hired by the Cotton Club; he composes "Creole Love Call."

1933—First tour of England; the orchestra plays at the prestigious London Palladium.

1935—His mother, Daisy Ellington, dies.

1936—The mayor of Los Angeles presents the keys to the city to Ellington, a rare honor for an African American at that time.

1937—His father, James Ellington, dies.

1939—Billy Strayhorn begins collaboration with Ellington.

1940—Billy Strayhorn composes "Take the 'A' Train," which replaces "East St. Louis Toodle-Oo" as the Ellington orchestra's theme song.

1943—Becomes first African-American to perform at Carnegie Hall in New York City, where he performs the long tone poem "Black, Brown, and Beige."

1956—Newport Jazz Festival gives Ellington new popularity; featured on the cover of *Time* magazine.

1959—Wins three Grammy awards for his first complete major film score, *Anatomy of a Murder*; records one copy of *The Queen's Suite* and sends it to Queen Elizabeth II in England.

1964—Mercer Ellington begins managing the Duke Ellington Orchestra.

1965—New York City gives Ellington a medal naming him "Musician of Every Year," distinguished composer, and worldwide ambassador of good will; Ellington presents first of three jazz concerts of Sacred Music in churches.

1967—Billy Strayhorn dies.

1969—President Richard Nixon awards him the Presidential Medal of Freedom—the nation's highest civilian honor—at Ellington's seventieth birthday party held at the White House.

1971—Becomes first performer and composer of popular music to be admitted to the Royal Swedish Academy of Music.

1974—Dies on May 24.

CHAPTER NOTES

Chapter 1

1. Studs Turkel, "Duke Ellington: Sounds of Life" in *Giants of Jazz* (New York: Harper Collins, 1975), p. 88.

2. John Edward Hasse, *Beyond Category: The Life and Genius of Duke Ellington* (New York: Simon & Schuster, 1993), p. 317.

3. Ibid.

4. Kent Smith, *Duke Ellington: Composer and Band Leader* (Los Angeles: Melrose Square, 1992), pp. 148–149.

5. Mercer Ellington with Stanley Dance, *Duke Ellington in Person: An Intimate Memoir*, (New York: Da Capo Press, 1978), pp. 111–112.

6. Smith, p. 149.

7. Hasse, p. 319.

8. Stanley Dance, *The World of Duke Ellington* (New York: Scribner, 1970), p. 173.

9. Ibid.

10. Bill Gutman, *Duke: the Musical Life of Duke Ellington* (New York: Random House, 1977), p. 133.

11. Hasse, pp. 320–321.

12. Ibid., p. 321.

13. Don George, *Sweet Man: The Real Duke Ellington* (New York: Putnam, 1981), p. 120.

14. Gutman, p. 135.

15. Hasse, p. 322.

Chapter 2

1. Duke Ellington, *Music Is My Mistress* (Garden City, N.Y.: Doubleday, Inc., 1973), p. 6.

2. Barry Ulanov, *Duke Ellington* (New York: Creative Age Press, 1946), pp. 4–5.

3. Duke Ellington, p. 9.

4. Ulanov, p. 3.

5. Geoffrey C. Ward, "Like His Music, the Duke Was Beyond Category," *Smithsonian*, May 1993, p. 64.

6. Ulanov, p. 3.

7. Mercer Ellington with Stanley Dance, *Duke Ellington in Person: An Intimate Memoir* (New York: Da Capo Press, 1978), p. 8.

8. Duke Ellington, p. 9.

9. John Edward Hasse, *Beyond Category: The Life and Genius of Duke Ellington* (New York: Simon & Schuster, 1993), p. 21.

10. Duke Ellington, p. 9.

11. Ulanov, p.7.

Chapter 3

1. Bill Gutman, *Duke: The Musical Life of Duke Ellington* (New York: Random House, 1977), p. 21.

2. Barry Ulanov, *Duke Ellington* (New York: Creative Age Press, 1946), p. 12.

3. Duke Ellington, *Music Is My Mistress* (Garden City, N.Y.: Doubleday, 1973), p. 19.

4. Ibid., p. 20.

5. Hugh McCarten, "A Synthesis of Sound," *Cobblestone: The History Magazine for Young People*, May 1993, p. 3.

6. Duke Ellington, p. 33.

7. Ibid., p. 26.

8. Ibid., p. 30.

9. Ulanov, p. 1.

10. Ibid., p. 2.

11. Ibid., p. 1.

12. Duke Ellington, p. 20.

13. Mercer Ellington with Stanley Dance, *Duke Ellington in Person: An Intimate Memoir* (New York: Da Capo Press, 1978), p. 19.

14. Duke Ellington, p. 22.

15. James Lincoln Collier, *Duke Ellington* (New York: Oxford University Press, 1987), p. 20.

16. Ulanov, p. 9.

17. Duke Ellington, p. 33.

18. Derek Jewell, *Duke: A Portrait of Duke Ellington* (New York: W.W. Norton & Company, 1977), p. 28.

19. Ibid., p. 29

20. Geoffrey C. Ward, "Like His Music, the Duke Was Beyond Category," *Smithsonian*, May 1993, p. 64.

Chapter 4

1. Duke Ellington, *Music Is My Mistress* (Garden City, N.Y.: Doubleday, 1973), p. 31.

2. John Edward Hasse, *Beyond Category: The Life and Genius of Duke Ellington* (New York: Simon & Schuster, 1993), p. 46.

3. Mark Tucker, *Ellington: The Early Years* (Urbana, Ill.: University of Illinois Press, 1991), p. 54.

4. Derek Jewell, *Duke: A Portrait of Duke Ellington* (New York: W.W. Norton & Company, 1977), p. 31.

5. Barry Ulanov, *Duke Ellington* (New York: Creative Age Press, 1946), p. 20.

6. Kent Smith, *Duke Ellington: Composer and Band Leader* (Los Angeles: Melrose Square, 1992), p. 46.

Chapter 5

1. Duke Ellington, *Music Is My Mistress* (Garden City, N.Y.: Doubleday, 1973), p. 69.

2. Mercer Ellington with Stanley Dance, *Duke Ellington in Person: An Intimate Memoir* (New York: Da Capo Press, 1978), p. 19.

3. Ibid., p. 15.

4. Kent Smith, *Duke Ellington: Composer and Band Leader* (Los Angeles: Melrose Square, 1992), p. 48.

5. Alistair Cooke, "The Grand Duke of Jazz," in *Fifty Who Made the Difference* (New York: Villard Books, 1984), p. 484.

6. Mercer Ellington, p. 19.

7. Smith, p. 52.

8. Ibid., p. 54.

9. John Edward Hasse, *Beyond Category: The Life and Genius of Duke Ellington* (New York: Simon & Schuster, 1993), p. 94.

10. Ibid., p. 91.

11. Duke Ellington, p. 73.

Chapter 6

1. Edwards Park, "Around the Mall and Beyond," *Smithsonian*, December 1993, p. 14.

2. Bill Gutman, *Duke: The Musical Life of Duke Ellington* (New York: Random House, 1977), p. 27.

3. Hugh McCarten, "A Synthesis of Sound," *Cobblestone: The History Magazine for Young People*, May 1993, pp. 3–4.

4. Kent Smith, *Duke Ellington: Composer and Band Leader* (Los Angeles: Melrose Square, 1992), p. 60.

5. Ibid., p. 187.

6. Whitney Balliett, "Jazz: Celebrating the Duke," *The New Yorker*, November 29, 1993, p. 136.

7. John Edward Hasse, *Beyond Category: The Life and Genius of Duke Ellington* (New York: Simon & Schuster, 1993), p. 102.

8. Geoffrey C. Ward, "Like His Music, the Duke Was Beyond Category," *Smithsonian*, May 1993, p. 72.

9. Ibid.

10. Alistair Cooke, "The Grand Duke of Jazz," in *Fifty Who Made the Difference* (New York: Villard Books, 1984), p. 484.

11. Ward, p. 66.

12. Hasse, p. 116.

13. Ibid.

14. Cleo Laine, in her introduction to the song just before performing it with the Duke Ellington Orchestra at Pier Six in Baltimore, Md., June 9, 1995.

Chapter 7

1. Geoffrey C. Ward, "Like His Music, the Duke Was Beyond Category," *Smithsonian*, May 1993, p. 66.
2. Ibid.
3. Ibid.
4. Kent Smith, *Duke Ellington: Composer and Band Leader* (Los Angeles: Melrose Square, 1992), p. 77.
5. "Stepping Out in Harlem," *Cobblestone: The History Magazine for Young People*, May 1993, p. 17.
6. Mercer Ellington with Stanley Dance, *Duke Ellington in Person: An Intimate Memoir* (New York: Da Capo Press, 1978), p. 8.
7. Joachim Ernst Berendt, *The Jazz Book: From Ragtime to Fusion and Beyond* (Brooklyn, N.Y.: Lawrence Hill Books, 1992), p. 78.
8. Ibid., pp. 78–79.
9. Smith, p. 79.
10. Ibid., p. 81.
11. Diana Childress, "Great and Glorious: Duke Ellington's Early Years," *Cobblestone: The History Magazine for Young People*, May 1993, p. 10.
12. Ward, p. 68.
13. Ibid., p. 70.
14. Ibid.
15. Smith, p. 77.
16. Ibid., p. 101.
17. Ibid.
18. Alistair Cooke, "The Grand Duke of Jazz," in *Fifty Who Made the Difference* (New York: Villard Books, 1984), p. 484.
19. Smith, p. 107.

Chapter 8

1. Kent Smith, *Duke Ellington: Composer and Band Leader* (Los Angeles: Melrose Square, 1992), p. 117.
2. Geoffrey C. Ward, "Like His Music, the Duke Was Beyond Category," *Smithsonian*, May 1993, p. 67.

3. Smith, p. 111.

4. Mercer Ellington with Stanley Dance, *Duke Ellington in Person: An Intimate Memoir* (New York: Da Capo Press, 1978), p. 88.

5. Kukula Glastris, "Dateline, the Duke Ellington Mystery," *U.S. News & World Report*, December 23, 1991, p. 17.

6. Mercer Ellington, interview with the author, June 9, 1995.

7. Smith, pp. 135–136.

8. Brandon Marie Miller, "A Musical Evolution: The Ellington Orchestra," *Cobblestone: The History Magazine for Young People*, May 1993, p. 25.

Chapter 9

1. Kent Smith, *Duke Ellington: Composer and Band Leader* (Los Angeles: Melrose Square, 1992), p. 131.

2. Brandon Marie Miller, "A Musical Evolution: The Ellington Orchestra," *Cobblestone: The History Magazine for Young People*, May 1993, p. 20.

3. Geoffrey C. Ward, "Like His Music, the Duke Was Beyond Category," *Smithsonian*, May 1993, p. 67.

4. Joachim Ernst Berendt, *The Jazz Book: From Ragtime to Fusion and Beyond* (Brooklyn, N.Y.: Lawrence Hill Books, 1992), p. 82.

5. Mercer Ellington with Stanley Dance, *Duke Ellington in Person: An Intimate Memoir* (New York: Da Capo Press, 1978), p. 138.

6. Mercer Ellington, interview with the author, June 9, 1995.

7. Alistair Cooke, "The Grand Duke of Jazz," in *Fifty Who Made the Difference* (New York: Villard Books, 1984), p. 485.

8. Joseph Hooper, "The Once and Future Duke," *Harper's Bazaar*, October 1993, p. 106.

9. Whitney Balliett, "Jazz: Celebrating the Duke," *The New Yorker*, November 29, 1993, p. 136.

Chapter 10

1. Kent Smith, *Duke Ellington: Composer and Band Leader* (Los Angeles: Melrose Square, 1992), p. 16.

2. Ibid., p. 11.

3. Ibid., p. 12.

4. John Edward Hasse, *Beyond Category: The Life and Genius of Duke Ellington* (New York: Simon & Schuster, 1993), p. 373.

5. Smith, pp. 159–160.

6. Brandon Marie Miller, "A Musical Evolution: The Ellington Orchestra," *Cobblestone: The History Magazine for Young People*, May 1993, p. 24.

7. Geoffrey C. Ward, "Like His Music, the Duke Was Beyond Category," *Smithsonian*, May 1993, p. 73.

8. Smith, p. 177.

9. Ward, p. 73.

10. Ibid.

11. Smith, p. 186.

12. Ibid.

13. Mercer Ellington, interview with the author, June 9, 1995.

14. Press sheet for the musical group Chicago, 1995.

15. Hasse, p. 18.

16. Joseph Hooper, "The Once and Future Duke," *Harper's Bazaar*, October 1993, p. 107.

FURTHER READING

Berendt, Joachim Ernst. *The Jazz Book: From Ragtime to Fusion and Beyond*. Brooklyn, N.Y.: Lawrence Hill Books, 1992.

Cobblestone: The History Magazine for Young People. May, 1993.

Ellington, Duke. *Music Is My Mistress*. Garden City, N.Y.: Doubleday, 1973.

Ellington, Mercer, with Stanley Dance. *Duke Ellington in Person: An Intimate Memoir*. New York: Da Capo Press, 1978.

Hasse, John Edward. *Beyond Category: The Life and Genius of Duke Ellington*. New York: Simon & Schuster, 1993.

Smith, Kent. *Duke Ellington: Composer and Band Leader*. Los Angeles: Melrose Square, 1992.

INDEX